# Missionary
# Earthkeeping

# Missionary Earthkeeping

Edited by
Calvin B. DeWitt and Ghillean T. Prance

Introduced by J. Mark Thomas

Mercer University Press
Macon, Georgia
1992

ISBN 0-86554-390-9 [casebound]          MUP/H318
ISBN 0-86554-404-2 [paperbound]          MUP/P96

BV
2063
· M564
1992

*Missionary Earthkeeping*
Copyright © 1992
Mercer University Press, Macon, GA 31207
All rights reserved
Printed in the United States of America


The paper used in this publication meets the minimum
requirements of American National Standard for Information
Sciences—Permanence of Paper for Printed Library Materials,
ANSI Z39.48–1984.


Library of Congress Cataloging-in-Publication Data

*Missionary earthkeeping*
/edited by Calvin B. DeWitt and Ghillean T. Prance;
introduced by J. Mark Thomas.
xii + 148 pp. Includes bibliographical references.
ISBN 0–86554–390–9 (Hard: alk. paper): $30.00.
ISBN 0–86554–404–2 (pbk.: alk. paper): $16.95.
1. Missions. 2. Human ecology—Religious aspects—
Christianity.
I. DeWitt, Calvin B. II. Prance, Ghillean T.,1937–
BV2063.M564 1992
266—dc20                                        92–42042
                                                       CIP

# Contents

# Preface

Even though the mission of the church is a saving one, Christian missions oftentimes have participated in the degradation of Creation. As essays in this volume will show, numerous instances are known: from monks in the Middle Ages who appeared "sometimes axe in hand, at the head of a troupe of believers scarcely converted, or of pagans surprised and indignant, to cut down the sacred trees, and thus root out popular superstition," to an early twentieth century Belgian Congo (Zaire) missionary who is reputed to have said, "I made up my mind that I would make it my work to bring the heathen out of the forest, to give them sunlight, to show them how to live in God's open world, to teach them to abandon this darkness. . . ." On the other hand, we also know of such persons as St. Francis, who modeled humility and respect for Creation; botanist missionary William Carey, who fostered a love for Creation and its keeping; early twentieth-century missionary Toyohiko Kagawa, who has influenced Japanese land reform and mountain reforestation; and Southern Baptist missionary Luther Copeland, who taught people to become priests of Creation and revere Creation as God's handiwork (Testerman).

In our day, mission programs that once condoned—or even promoted—destruction of Creation are being propelled into a new awareness that comes from the interplay of increasing environmental degradation and biblical teachings on the care and keeping of Creation. Once having no grasp of how human beings could command sufficient power to threaten Creation, the church and its Christian missions are for the first time coming to fathom the profound meaning of Revelation 11:18: "The time has come . . . for destroying those who destroy the earth." We are altering the energy relationship between Earth and Sun; we are losing topsoil and desertifying the land at unprecedented rates; we are widely deforesting the land, and consequent floods and droughts bring increased hunger and sewage-borne disease; we are extinguishing at least three kinds of plants and animals every day; we are contaminating surface and ground waters world-wide, especially amongst the poor; we are injecting trouble-some materials into global circulations of water and air; and we are extinguishing indigenous knowledge of the medicinal, food, and fiber uses of thousands of species of plants and animals, as well as indigenous wisdom on sustainable living.

Accompanying this destruction and defilement is the muting of Creation's testimony. In many urban areas Psalm 19:1 has become meaningless—the heavens that declare God's glory no longer can be seen. The proclamation of Romans 1:20, that Creation's testimony to God's divinity and everlast-ing power leaves all people without excuse, rings hollow.

Christian missions have been forced into new perspec-tives. We who bring the good news of God's love for the cosmos (John 3:16) and of Jesus Christ's work as Creator, sustainer, and reconciler (John 1; Col 1; Heb 1) cannot be complicit bystanders or participants in the degradation and defilement of the world God creates, loves, sustains, and re-conciles. Rather than destroying the groves to prove that "our God reigns," we find ourselves moving to preserve and re-store God's world, to bring honor and glory to our Creator, and to restore the full force of Creation's evangelical testimo-ny to God's divinity, steadfast love, sustaining power, and pervasive reconciliation. Imaging God, we find that we too must love the world, care for the earth, and bring reconcilia-tion to Creation. Following God's command in Genesis 2:15, we find that we must *keep* the Garden. Just as the word "keep" in the Aaronic Blessing ("The Lord bless you and *keep* you," Num 6:24) means a loving, caring, sustaining "keep-ing," so it does in Genesis 2:15. Our keeping of Creation must be loving, caring, and sustaining; it must be a Christian earthkeeping that honors the One through whom all things were made, the One through whom all things hold together, and the One through whom all things are reconciled.

What is "missionary earthkeeping"? It is mission work that honestly acts upon a full understanding of Creation, of its degradation, and of biblical principles for its proper care and keeping. It is enterprise whose goal is the wholeness, integrity, and renewal of people and Creation and their relationships with each other and the Creator; it is reconciliation of *all things* (1 Cor 15:20-22; Col 1:15-20; Rom 5).

This book, *Missionary Earthkeeping*, originates from a paper by the same title presented by Ghillean Prance at one of the annual Au Sable Forums at the Au Sable Institute of Environmental Studies. Soon thereafter the title of this paper was selected as the topic for an entire Au Sable Forum, and over the next two years the world was searched for missionaries who practiced missionary earthkeeping. These missionaries were invited to come together to discuss their work; this volume is the result. The editors and the authors intend it as a source of encouragement and incentive to all who are working in the mission field to join biblical teachings on earthkeeping with ecological knowledge to bring Good News to the world—Good News that announces and honors God and Jesus Christ as Creator, sustainer, and reconciler of all things.

Au Sable Institute is here acknowledged for its support for the Forum from which this book is derived and for support for the preparation and publication of the manuscript. The New York Botanical Garden is also acknowledged, particularly Frances "Mickey" Maroncelli who assisted in communications and organization of the Forum while Ghillean Prance served there as Senior Vice-President for Science and Director of the Institute for Economic Botany. Also acknowledged is the invaluable and selfless service of J. Mark Thomas, Senior Research Fellow of Au Sable Institute and accomplished scholar and writer in social and environmental ethics. He worked closely and continuously with the editors through all phases of the preparation of the manuscript, including text -reading, editing, correspondence, and proofreading. Without his energetic work and devotion to this task, this book would not have been produced. The Au Sable Institute has conducted the Au Sable Forums since 1980, bringing theologians, scientists, and laypersons together to explore the relationships between the scriptures and environment, between Christianity and ecology. Numerous articles and books have resulted. Most people who write about Christianity and ecology have come to Au Sable Institute—as Forum participants, as professors, as students—and many of them consider this place as a kind of second home. Through the Institute's association with some eighty evangelical Christian colleges in the United States and Canada and by its associations with Christian and religious leaders worldwide, it has provided a locus for the integration of faith and learning on matters relating to the integrity of Creation.

Thanks must be extended to all who have contributed to the Au Sable Forums from which a base of knowledge has been steadily building, and particularly to the authors who have contributed to this book. Thanks also are due to the Board of Trustees of the Institute for supporting this project through a generous Trustees Grant, namely Orin G. Gelderloos, John D. Loeks, Ross S. Whaley, Bert Froysland, Rolf Bouma, Job Ebenezer, John Olmstead, Ghillean T. Prance, Harold Z. Snyder, and J. Elliott Corbett. Finally, thanks to Mercer University Press and its staff for publishing this work.

Calvin B. DeWitt
Waubesa Marsh
Town of Dunn, Wisconsin

Ghillean T. Prance
Royal Botanical Gardens
Kew Green, England
October 23, 1992

# About the Contributors

**Robert Clobus**, SMA, born in the Netherlands, has worked extensively in Ghana since his ordination into the Catholic priesthood in 1926, with a two-year hiatus for environmental studies in the Philippines, Tanzania, and Kenya. At present he is the coordinator and priest leader in a church-related environmental project on the Afram Plains in the Ashanti region of Ghana.

**Calvin B. DeWitt** (Ph.D., University of Michigan) is Professor of Environmental Studies at the University of Wisconsin, Madison, and Director of the Au Sable Institute of Environmental Studies in Mancelona, Michigan. An internationally recognized expert in wetlands, hunger, and sustainability, he has pioneered in the issues of Christian environmental stewardship. One of his more recent publications in this developing field is *The Environment and the Christian: What Can We Learn from the New Testament?* (which he edited and to which he contributed).

**James W. Gustafson** (Ph.D. candidate, University of Wisconsin, Madison) is presently the President of Issan Development Foundation in Udon Thani, Thailand, an organization that he founded in 1983. He also holds masters degrees from Fuller Seminary in divinity and applied anthropology. He has been working in Thailand since 1971 to establish sustainable forms of agriculture and ecological models for mission.

**Mutombo Mpanya** (Ph.D., University of Michigan) is Professor of Environmental Science at World College West in Petaluma, California. From 1972 to 1976 he was the Associate Director of the Menno Central Committee, Zaire, and was responsible for doing project impact analysis. Since 1977 he has been the Associate Director of the African Institute at the University of Notre Dame, where he trains church and lay workers to work in environmental projects in Africa. He was a faculty fellow at the Kellog Institute of Notre Dame University from 1984 to 1988, where he coordinated the program of private voluntary organizations, concentrating on food production.

**Ghillean T. Prance**, M.A., D.Phil., Fil. Dr., F.L.S., is currently the Director of the Royal Botanical Gardens at Kew, in his native England. He came to this post from The New York Botanical Garden, where he had served in a number of capacities since 1963. A prolific author in plant systematics, plant ecology, ethnobotany, and conservation, he has spent over eight years in field work and botanical exploration in Amazonian Brazil.

**Dennis E. Testerman** (M.Div., Southeastern Baptist Theological Seminary) is a Resource Conservation Specialist for the Cabarrus Soil and Water Conservation District in Concord, North Carolina. In addition to his seminary degree, he has a B.S. in forestry, with an environmental conservation emphasis. He worked for three years in mission posts in Nigeria and Pakistan, where his interest in the relationship between ecology and missions flowered.

**J. Mark Thomas** is a social ethicist (Ph.D., University of Chicago). He conducts research and writes on issues of sociology, ethics, and theology as a Senior Research Fellow at Au Sable Institute of Environmental Studies. A number of his books and articles have focused on the normative meaning of scientific and technological progress. He also teaches sociology at the community college in Madison, Wisconsin.

# Introduction

## by J. Mark Thomas

When William Carey accepted the great commission to evangelize the world, he carried to Asia a deep concern for biblical religion and for the care of the Earth. Early in the nineteenth century, however, the idea of a "world" was still "a matter of daring anticipation or utopian vision."[1] Carey and those who followed in the early modern missionary movement evangelized still-distinct areas of the globe that maintained large degrees of independence from one another. But, by 1945 two world wars and a transnational economic depression had made concrete the reality of a "world"—an interrelatedness of all human groups. None could escape the repercussions of actions by others distant in space and culture.[2]

Now, as the twentieth century moves to a close, the "world" that theologian Paul Tillich saw emerging from the ashes of the Second World War has taken on a more tragic reality. While the atomic age was just dawning then, it is now taken for granted that losing the "balance of nuclear terror" will result in world conflagration. If the problem had been to control the Promethean forces of technology and the world-market system, it now has become one of planetary survival. If all aspects of culture—religion, politics, education, intellectual, and economic life—were bending under the developing technological civilization, today no human culture on the globe escapes its reach.

New to the contemporary situation is the degradation of the environment that today unites the world by mutual threat. While less dramatic than the nuclear menace, environmental damage contains the quiet peril of destroying the conditions for life on the planet. Because ecological threats have the character of slow strangulation rather than sudden death, they are the more insidious and dangerous. They can be ignored or denied until the planetary victim is beyond help. Powerful economic, political, and cultural interests, for the sake of short-term gains, can build temporary refuge from global repercussions until ultimate destruction is inevitable.

Environmental degradation, nevertheless, has confirmed that an interrelated "world" has come into being. Notions of national sovereignty developed during the eighteenth and nineteenth centuries have become anachronistic when describing the contemporary situation. Actions can no longer be assumed to have only localized and short-term effects: emissions from industries in the United States now degrade Canadian lakes and forests in the form of acid rain; release of chlorofluorocarbons around the globe destroys Earth's ozone layer; clear-cutting of tropical forests reduces the mass of $CO_2$-consuming plants; the burning of fossil fuels releases in a geological moment the carbon stored for centuries; effluvia from factories in every industrialized nation are carried by rivers to the ocean, where they destroy plant and animal life by poisoning their environments. Nations, if yet sovereign in action, are no longer autonomous in effect. Indeed, they impose the potential for global degradation on all others.

Likewise, the world-market system dominant in Western nations in 1945 now penetrates every nation and group. Traditional societies have been woven into its matrix, as have erstwhile communist countries (even before *glasnost*). The Polish golf cart imported into the United States was not made for local consumption; the Poles do not yet play golf. Worldwide agencies such as the International Monetary Fund grant low-interest loans to developing countries, but with conditions that narrow the range of options for deeply indebted nations. "Development" has come to mean a progressive entry into a modern market economy, producing not for subsistence but for trade—by industrializing, urbanizing, selling off raw materials, and developing cheap, landless, and industrious labor. Agribusiness means all-season fresh food for the First World. Even nations experiencing domestic hunger and starvation export food for the international market. The world has become dominated by corporations with budgets exceeding those of some nations. An analysis of the impact of multinational corporations on Third World development more than a decade ago remains valid today: the net effect is to increase hunger and poverty and to widen the gap between rich and poor, both nationally and internationally.[3]

Whatever their merits or demerits, however, world market and technological systems have become more pervasive than could have been imagined. In fact, Tillich believed that the destructiveness unleased by these forces had made it impossible for the people of the postwar world to put their faith in them again. Surveying the situation in 1945, Tillich asked how the Christian church might respond. He cautioned that no one group, nation, or singularly theoretical or practical approach could embrace and reply to the world situation.

> The more a Christian group embraces elements from all these different aspects of the present world, the more adequately will it comprehend the true questions and formulate right answers. This means that the Christian church can speak authoritatively and effectively to our world today only as it is truly . . . universal.[4]

This, then, is the new situation that all groups—secular and Christian—and world missions face today. World *missions* has become *world* missions. This volume represents an attempt to develop an understanding of this newly emerging world situation, especially as it is manifest in ecological threat. For Christian missions, it offers some answers to this situation from diverse elements of the church worldwide. The five contributors to this work represent five different Christian traditions—Catholic and Protestant, First World and Third World, missionary and academic. They do not share a common theology or ideological commitment. Rather, each is struggling with the problems of Christian mission to the developing world in the light of the ecological and world situation. All are concerned with the meaning of "missionary earthkeeping."

What is most striking is not the utter pluralism of their accounts. Rather, it is that despite very real differences in origin and viewpoint, they analyze both the situation and the needs it engenders in remarkably consistent fashion. What all five of these authors share is their Christian faith and a similar experience of the problems they are facing. Their analyses and actions emerge not merely from the theoretical distance of the classroom, but from interaction with those whose lives are most affected by what they do. Thus, while these contributors abide by the canons of responsible contemporary scholarship, their tone and style are generally personal and involved. Without an apparent conscious design to do so, each of the authors attends to the interaction of faith and practice—to new and renewed relationships to nature in response to the emerging world.

On the basis of academic research and his experience as a Southern Baptist missionary, Dennis Testerman opens the conversation by reviewing the ecological effects of the two primary phases of missionary activity in Africa and Asia: from the Roman Empire through the Middle Ages and from William Carey's Baptist Missionary Society in 1792 to the present. In doing so, Testerman reveals the ambiguity of missionary work to date, its ecological successes and failures. From the monk's felling sacred trees and draining swamps to the modern missionaries' cutting trees and organizing monocultures to serve the market, Testerman documents the destruction caused by Christian missions. Still, the environmental knowledge and sensitivity of some Christian missionaries are also noted, from St. Francis to Toyohiko Kagawa. Testerman draws an interesting contrast between the Benedictine tendency to subdue nature and the Franciscan charge to let it be, but recommends that these two traditions "be held in tension, while recognizing that in the past the Benedictine approach has predominated." While no one model may be appropriate for all settings, he concedes, Christian missions should take seriously the charge to tend and keep the garden, including the way it organizes its own missions and camps. "Just as during the 'Dark Ages' monks witnessed to 'barbarians' and strove to wipe out 'paganism,' so also missionaries of the colonial period, traveling to 'the Dark Continent,' sought to deliver the 'natives' from 'primitive' religions," notes Testerman. He further contends that "such pejorative terms, used far too frequently in Christian missions, betray an arrogance that can thwart effective proclamation of the gospel." This theme is echoed by the other essays in this volume

Ghillean T. Prance, ethnobotanist, Amazonian explorer, and director of the Royal Botanic Gardens in Kew, England, maintains that without "a deep understanding of the culture in which we are working, it is easy to bring North American and European culture rather than or as well as a true faith." Instead of leading to "an ultimate pluralism of religious values," however, Prance's argument portends that "the ecology of indigenous peoples and of their reverence for nature can lead to the establishment of a much more permanent and environmentally sound Christian faith." In the process, Prance criticizes styles of missionary activity that have emphasized clearing more land, offering more products for sale on the market, or moving into settled communities near a fixed church. Such practices have resulted not only in the diminution of native practice, but sometimes in the destruction of the land and even the extinction of the native peoples themselves. In contrast, many traditional practices of "agroforestry"—including the maintenance of biological diversity, fallowing, ritual tree planting, cultural traditions regarding food gathering, holding common goods, and the planting of useful vegetation along trails—not only provide adequately for native people, but preserve the environment through the generations. These latter traditions, Prance contends, coincide with biblical teachings. Missionary earthkeepers thus must learn, respect, and preserve those ecological traditions of native people that honor creation, even as they bring them the message of the gospel.

Robert Clobus, a Catholic missionary with the Society of African Missions, portrays a deteriorating ecological situation in the West African nation of Ghana. There, a population that has doubled in size in fifty years has put pressure on the land to produce yearly, thus eliminating traditional fallow times. It has also contributed to the clearing of tropical forests to provide more arable land, with the effect of deforestation and the exhaustion of the fragile tropical soils. Mechanized farming has overcultivated the soil, changing even its texture (especially its water-holding characteristics). Firewood has become scarce. Few farmers own their own land. Further, draught in the Sahel region of West Africa reduces the fertility of the area. Although periods of drought are climatically normal for this region, it may be that human action contributes to their length and severity. Overgrazing and overcultivation during rainy periods, for instance, reduce the ground cover and may exacerbate drought through biogeophysical mechanisms. Ghana's traditional subsistence economy has been replaced by a money economy, with a consequent focus upon cash crops.

Clobus argues that such environmental degradation could be minimized by practices of "ecofarming," in which "the demands made on the earth are compensated by the goods returned to her." Traditional Ghanian religious and cultural practices tended to support the ecological treatment of land, Traditional land ownership, however,—with its subsequent rights and obligations—has given way to the concentration of property in the hands of the few and powerful. Clobus asks that all the churches in Ghana identify with the poor and dispossessed of that country and provide resources for agroforestry and ecofarming, thereby ameliorating the "ill-conceived economic development" that contributes to environmental destruction.

Mutombo Mpanya's case study shifts the focus of the conversation from corporate and societal considerations to the environmental effects of Christian missions themselves. He demonstrates that a church project, by its physical presence, evangelization, and educational programs, may contribute to ecological crises that threaten the life of a local African community. His methodical study of three sites indicates that there has been ecological destruction around mission stations, due in large part to their ecological and educational practices. They introduced private property and new methods of tree removal, built modern buildings requiring great amounts of local materials, increased the consumption of firewood, and taught Western materialism while devaluing the ecological orientation of local religions and of traditional agricultural education. The ironic result is that the Christian missions hurt those they have come to save. Are there no better ways to evangelize?

The final essay in this volume explores a model for missions that has the promise of integrating ecological, spiritual, and economic development. Its focus is mission to whole persons and the whole of creation. As a Swedish Evangelical Covenant missionary to Thailand, James W. Gustafson had designed "integrated holistic development" to realize progressively what persons, communities, and churches might be in the light of the gospel. His essay outlines seven steps, or principles, guiding such development:

1. Know the message of the gospel.
2. Know the local people and the local culture.

3. Contextualize the message of the gospel.
4. Confront the value system of the local culture with that of the gospel.
5. Establish dynamic equivalent churches in the local culture.
6. Establish socioeconomic projects in dynamic equivalent churches.
7. Enable the church to do integrated holistic development in its own community.

Additionally, Gustafson provides an invaluable set of appendixes demonstrating the practical design of his mission, including the Farm, the Center, and the Foundation. Here is a working ecological mission, a practical manifestation of earthkeeping. Local species of plants and animals are cultivated in ecological interdependence to form an economic and resource base. Churches develop indigenous leadership that becomes self-sustaining and fosters church growth. Economic dependence is turned into economic independence through carefully designed development programs.

As Gustafson would be the first to point out, however, his design cannot be transported intact to any other setting; it is specifically fashioned for northeast Thailand. Every mission aspiring to integrated holistic development must be geared to local culture. Yet, Gustafson's work is a paradigm for the kinds of ecological wisdom that can express the theological concern for creation, for human development, and for embodying the grace of God.

The world situation near the close of this millennium is desperate. The hope engendered by the opening up of Eastern Europe is diminished by the seriousness of the ecological threat there. The growing public awareness of the necessity of tending the Earth is offset by the continued power of social, political, and economic forces that militate against actually doing so. The degradation of the web of water, air, soil, and human systems that make up the Earth is being investigated and resisted, but some forms of damage will require decades or centuries to repair if they can be repaired at all. Nuclear war seems less likely in the post cold war world, but war preparations still steal from the poor, while conventional fighting undermines the life-supporting ecosystem.

The great question now facing humankind is whether the necessary moral and spiritual courage can be mustered to alter the trajectory of destruction before the Earth's environmental systems are stressed beyond saving. In some ways, the question is new, because human actions never before had the capacity to threaten the very basis for life itself. But, in a significant sense, this question has always been before those who would be Earthkeepers: "This day I call heaven and earth as witnesses against you that I have set before you life and death, blessings and curses" (Deut 30:19a). It is the call of the church to choose life in the midst of the threat of death. It is the burden of missionary earthkeepers to actualize the meaning of the gospel, not merely that Christians might live, but that the whole world might realize what it was created to be. "Now choose life, so that you and your children may live" (Deut 30:19b).

# Notes

[1]Paul Tillich, *The Spiritual Situation in Our Technical Society*, ed. J. Mark Thomas (Macon, GA: Mercer University Press, 1988), 3.

[2]Ibid.

[3]Richard J. Barnet and Ronald E. Müller, *Global Reach: The Power of the Multinational Corporations* (New York: Simon and Schuster, 1974). A reconsideration and update of the issue of this volume is currently under way at Barnet's Institute for Policy Studies in Washington, D.C.

[4]Tillich, *Spiritual Situation*, 39.

# Chapter 1

# Missionary Earthkeeping: Glimpses of the Past, Visions of the Future

*by Dennis E. Testerman*

Wherever Christian missionaries have journeyed around the world, they have gone as agents of civilization. With evangelistic zeal, they have transformed not only human lives but also the land. Such impact on the environment has been both constructive and destructive.

A frequent step in the process of evangelization throughout missions history has been the effort to wipe out all vestiges of local religion. Unless a religious void was presumed to exist, evangelists often set out to create one. Land clearing produced another kind of void, making way for mission centers and food production. In some instances, efforts to eradicate both religion and vegetation coalesced in a single act—the cutting down of sacred groves.

Missionaries historically have directly affected the land as they worked in agriculture to increase crop production. Clearing and cultivating the land were common activities of monastic missionaries during the Middle Ages as they traveled across the Roman Empire and eventually to the most remote regions of Europe. In the modern period, missionaries were closely allied with the colonialists who went forth from Europe to other continents, exploring and exploiting the natural resources of those lands.

Similarities between the attitudes and actions of the medieval monks and those of colonial-era missionaries in Africa are particularly evident. Just as during the "Dark Ages" monks witnessed to "barbarians" and strove to wipe out "paganism," so also missionaries of the colonial period, traveling to "the Dark Continent," sought to deliver the "natives" from "primitive" religions.[1] Such pejorative terms, used far too frequently in Christian missions, betray an arrogance that can thwart effective proclamation of the gospel.

Arrogance also lurks behind the assumption that humanity is the sole object of God's concern. This attitude results in a rift between humanity and the rest of creation, producing a false sense of independence on the part of humans. Everything that God created was declared good (Gen 1:1–31), but now the whole creation suffers degeneration as a consequence of humankind's broken covenant with God. Thus, the entire created order becomes the object of God's salvific activity. The divine work of creating and redeeming is one work. All of creation groans in agony awaiting redemption by God (Rom 8:22–23), longing for healing and wholeness, for shalom in the fullest sense of the word.

The focus of this discussion about missionary earthkeeping is on two historical periods: the age of Christian expansion at the end of the Roman Empire through the Middle Ages, and the modern missionary period as inaugurated by William Carey with the formation of the Baptist Missionary Society in 1792. Illustrations of missionary earthkeeping during the latter period highlight two continents—Africa and Asia—due to the experience and interests of the writer.

Because of a long-standing personal interest in trees and a belief in their importance to soil and water conservation, examples in this chapter of both positive and negative missionary impact on the environment will center on the theme of trees. Ironically, my own involvement in missions has been through the vehicle of agriculture, owing to the scarcity of requests for missionary foresters or conservationists. The legacy of soil erosion, desertification, and related environmental damage left by large-scale land clearing and other ecologically unsound agricultural practices is lamentable. The idea that agricultural missionaries must join with other missionaries in working toward a just and sustainable agriculture will be supported later in this discussion by the insights of missionaries, theological educators, and others committed to earthkeeping.

Finally, the chapter explores the need for sensitizing all missionaries to environmental issues and examines some directions that education for Christian earthkeeping might take. The perspective for this final section is that of my personal pilgrimage and sense of being called to preach and embody good news to the whole creation.

## Monasticism and Missions in the Middle Ages

From Jerusalem, the gospel message spread across the face of the Earth. Early Christians overcame many obstacles —including persecution—as they crossed cultural, racial, national, and geographical barriers. Some of these barriers disappeared with the designation of Constantine—a confessing Christian—as the sole emperor of Rome in 323. Under his governance, Christianity's status changed to that of a state religion. Since that time, the spread of Christianity has been closely allied first with imperialistic and, later, with nationalistic expansion.

Monasticism became the main channel of the church's missionary activity from the late Roman Empire through the Middle Ages.[2] Most of this activity centered in Europe, with the monks following the Roman soldiers into conquered territories. They also went beyond the bounds of the empire as pioneers to more remote regions of Europe and to other continents—particularly Asia and northern Africa. The fall of the Roman Empire in the fifth century and subsequent waves of invasion by Germanic tribes marked the beginning of the Middle Ages.

A popular theory among some Christians today regarding the cause of the Roman Empire's collapse rests on a perceived decline in Roman morality. A more critical factor, however, may have been the large number of nonproductive members of that society, especially in the army and the governmental bureaucracy, both of which increased greatly in size after the third century. In the Christian sector, monks often were net consumers rather than producers, adding to the total demand for food and other resources.[3] This trend would change in some religious orders as the place of work in the monastic life-style and routine was elevated, particularly under the influence of St. Benedict.

Many monks in the Middle Ages were extremely zealous in carrying out their Christian mission. Their enthusiasm in rooting out all expressions of polytheism corresponds to the Crusaders' fervor in combating Islam during the church's second millennium. Montalembert, in his two-volume work entitled *Monks of the West*, notes that the monks would appear "sometimes axe in hand, at the head of a troupe of believers scarcely converted, or of pagans surprised and indignant, to cut down the sacred trees, and thus root out the popular superstition."[4]

## The Benedictines

One of the earliest and most influential monastic movements was formed in the sixth century by Benedict of Nursia. In establishing a monastery at Monte Cassino, Benedict set a precedent by destroying a sacred grove on the mountain's summit. On the site of the former grove, he built two chapels for the Christian worship of God.[5]

Boniface, a Benedictine living during the eighth century, followed Benedict's example by felling the sacred oak of Thor at Geismar in Hesse. The lumber from this tree was then used in the construction of a chapel in honor of St. Peter. Stephen Neill, in his *History of Christian Missions*, notes the frequency of such destruction of sacred groves, yet offers the following defense: "This must not be taken as a manifestation of brutal violence, or disregard of the feelings of the local population. The act was akin to the trial by ordeal, which was part of the tradition of the northern nations; it was, in fact, a conflict not between men but between the gods."[6] Neill maintains that the onlookers readily believed the truth of Boniface's religious claims upon the felling of the oak, because the monk boldly defied the locally revered deity with impunity.

A more prudent approach to that of direct action was the persuasion practiced by St. Sturm, a pupil of Boniface. Rather than laying an axe to the tree himself, he preached to the yet-unconverted people that they should cut down their sacred groves and build churches in their place.[7]

Along with the monks' desire to witness to their faith in one God, monastic beliefs about physical labor and the restoration of earthly paradise influenced their relationship to the environment. A unique emphasis of Benedict's Rule was its focus on work as a form of worship. For Benedict and his followers, work—especially manual labor—was an act of prayer. Benedict stated that "idleness is an enemy of the soul."[8] The early monks seem to have understood their labors as the exercise of dominion over the rest of the created order. In establishing and maintaining monastic settlements throughout Europe, medieval monks envisioned themselves as partners with God. According to Clarence Glacken in his book *Traces on the Rhodian Shore*, "There was often a deep feeling among the monks that in their forest retreats, their clearings, their tillage, they were duplicating conditions like those of paradise before the fall."[9] Regrettably, the monks apparently overlooked that paradise, as portrayed in Genesis, was an efficient food-production system dominated by tree crops and characterized by rich diversity. Greater fruitfulness and long-term benefits to the land could have been achieved by the monks through cooperating with creation (of which humans are an integral part), rather than imposing upon it a human sense of order.

Such labors undoubtedly resulted in short-term improvement in the quality of human life, one example being the reduced incidence of water-borne disease as swamps were drained.[10] The monks also made valuable contributions in reclaiming land damaged by the ravages of successive invasions of tribal groups that had swept across Europe.[11] The forests were not inexhaustible, however, and in time they became scarce in various regions of the European continent.[12] Changes in the European landscape were accelerated with the acquisition of additional monastic property.

By the ninth century, "the abbot found himself the lord over large estates worked by dependent peasants."[13] The church came to be the greatest landed institution of the Middle Ages. "In a system fundamentally and almost entirely agricultural, possession of the soil gave great possibilities of influence and power, and during these centuries the Benedictine monasteries were among the largest holders of arable lands."[14] Land was leased out by the monasteries to be worked by serfs as the monastic landholdings increased. In three-centuries' time, Benedictine monks had become an elite, noble class "supported by the labor of serfs on their estates, while they devoted themselves to educational and liturgical work."[15]

## *The Cistercians*

Departures such as these from Benedict's Rule led to corruption and to exploitation of people and land, on the one hand, and to various reform movements on the other. The reforms of Cluny in 910 and that of Citeaux in 1098 were the most significant of such movements. With time the Cluniac monasteries themselves became centers of wealth, again separating them from the ideal of St. Benedict, a development due in part to the elevation of worship over work and study.[16]

The Cistercian order founded at Citeaux became one of the most significant monastic orders of the late Middle Ages. This reform movement represented a drastic break with Cluniac monasticism and a return to the foundations of the Benedictine order. The Cistercians figured as prominently during the late Middle Ages as had the Benedictines in the early medieval period in the picture of civilization in general—and resource management in particular.[17] The work of the Cistercians in the draining of swamps and marshlands is especially noteworthy.

## *Employment of Lay Brothers*

The capacity of monastic orders for changing the landscape increased not only with the accumulation of property, but also through the employment of lay brothers. These workers were enlisted from the peasants who followed the pioneering monks across Europe. The resultant collaboration is portrayed in a twelfth-century illustration depicting an oak tree being felled by a monk even as a lay brother works to remove its branches.[18] In his book *Medieval Village, Manor, and Monastery*, G. G. Coulton goes so far as to give these lay brothers, rather than the monks, credit for much of the land development that took place during the Middle Ages. He asserts, "The peasants not only saw that the monk had ceased to labour, but they also knew the monk was an 'outsider,' a sportsman, and perhaps one who rode over their own crops."[19]

One positive side of this delegation of labor to others was that the monks gained time for study. They were observers of the natural world and sought to interpret what they saw and experienced. Thus, the monasteries came to be centers of botanical knowledge. St. John Gualberto, founder of the Vallumbrosan Order, sought to preserve forested land not suitable for cultivation and actively practiced reforestation techniques. His followers were sought out as university faculty members because of their wisdom and skill in forest culture. In time, even the Benedictine monks of Monte Cassino came to appreciate the vulnerability of the forests. Some six centuries after St. Benedict cleared the sacred groves to found his order, the abbot of Monte Cassino decreed that the forest was the property of the abbey and that his permission was required for all hunting and timber-cutting activity.[20]

## Francis and Benedict—Models for Earthkeeping?

In contrast to the interventionism of the Benedictines and Cistercians, St. Francis's reverent and humble attitude toward nature merits him the status of "patron saint of ecologists" in the opinion of Lynn White, Jr. In his essay, "The Historical Roots of Our Ecological Crisis," White asserts that "the victory of Christianity over paganism was the greatest psychic revolution in the history of our culture."[21] He continues, "By destroying pagan animism, Christianity made it possible to exploit nature in a mood of indifference to the feelings of natural objects."[22] Lamenting the rate and extent of environmental destruction today, White reflects: "To a Christian a tree can be no more than a physical fact. The whole concept of a sacred grove is alien to Christianity and to the ethos of the West. For nearly two millennia Christian missionaries have been chopping down sacred groves. . . ."[23]

For the profoundly religious problem of the exploitation of the Earth, White offers a religious solution: he calls for an alternative Christian understanding of the relationship of humanity to the rest of creation. White bases this new understanding on the life of St. Francis. Recognizing Francis's difference from other monks of the Middle Ages, including Benedict, White dubs Francis "the greatest radical since Christ."[24] The essence of this alternative view is that all aspects of nature are spiritually autonomous or, in other words, all creatures are equal. This position, according to White, was predicated upon Francis's "belief in . . .

humility—not merely for the individual but for [humankind] as a species."[25] Evidence of this humility is found in St. Francis's attitude toward Muslims. Stephen Neill believes that while virtually all of Christendom was engaged in a crusade to enslave or exterminate the followers of Mohammed, Francis may have been the first Christian to reach out to them with respect. Francis thought that the Muslims' continued unbelief indicated that "the Gospel had not been presented to them in its simplicity and beauty."[26] Acting on this belief, Francis traveled to the Muslim territories of Morocco, Spain, and Egypt on successive journeys. On the latter trip, Francis gained an audience with the sultan, who "seems to have shown marked deference to Francis." For the following two centuries the Franciscans, along with the Dominicans, were the primary channels of missionary outreach.[27] The Franciscans helped bring vitality and a greater evangelical focus to the missionary efforts of the period.[28]

René Dubos—the renowned scientist, philosopher, and author—counters White's advocacy of Francis as patron saint of ecologists by proposing Benedict "as a patron saint of those who believe that true conservation means not only protecting nature against human misbehavior but also developing human activities which favor a creative, harmonious relationship between [humanity] and nature."[29] He believes that Benedict's Rule promotes the concept of stewardship as found in Genesis 2:15.[30] Dubos contrasts this active intervention in the environment with St. Francis's more passive reverence for nature.

He offers the reader a personal insight into why he is uncomfortable with the "unworldly" attitude of St. Francis. By his own admission, Dubos prefers "to impose [his] own sense of order upon natural processes."[31] In contrast, the way of St. Francis is not that of imposition, but rather the way of cooperation and persuasion. Francis's simple life-style of service to the poor had minimal negative impact on the environment. His humble example was an alternative to the arrogance of the church of his day. "All too rare in the history of missions, he seems literally to have believed that the gospel is God's good news to 'the whole creation' and not just to us human beings."[32]

Rather than choose sides in the White-Dubos debate, I would recommend that the Franciscan and Benedictine traditions be held in tension, while recognizing that in the past the Benedictine approach has predominated. Missionaries today would do well to look to Francis as a model of humility and of respect both for the environment and for other cultures and religions. Agricultural missionaries in particular should critically assess Dubos's enthusiastic endorsement of Benedictine-style aggressive intervention in nature. But ultimately, perhaps we need both the "contemplative Franciscan spirit" and the Benedictine "activist spirit."[33] To protect endangered environments in the face of humanity's ever-growing capacity for their destruction requires activism channeled in the direction of conservation and preservation.

## Missionaries and Earthkeeping in the Modern Era

As evangelization and civilization accompanied each other in Europe from the time of the Roman Empire through the Middle Ages, the same was true when Christians went to the uttermost ends of the Earth during the modern missionary period. Stephen Neill makes a correlation between the church's early expansion and the missionary activity of the last 200 years, stating that "civilization meant Roman civilization; and hand in hand with civilization went the Church, which was the heir of the ancient world. As in many parts of Africa today, any[one] who wished to be regarded as civilized was almost bound to become a Christian."[34]

During the 1800s in Europe, the church and the business community had a growing interest in Africa. Missionary and colonial efforts were often companion  enterprises. In his book *Modern Africa: Change and Continuity*, Richard Hull summarizes this period:

> In much of tropical Africa, the missionaries, not the European traders and enclave administrators, were the torchbearers of Western influence until at least the early 1890s. . . . From about 1875, missionary propaganda gave imperialism an undeserved moral justification. The Christian missionaries, with their denominational varieties and rivalries, undermined traditional social, religious, and political institutions and obscured true European intentions. This made African leaders even more vulnerable to imperial conquest. In many ways, the missionaries paved the way for European colonialism.[35]

## David Livingstone

One such pathfinder was David Livingstone, the noted missionary-explorer who navigated the Zambesi River to the center of the African continent. Before his time, few had dared to penetrate the awesome continent with its thick jungles along the coasts. Livingstone envisioned his explorations as preparing the way for the establishment of "centers of Christianity and civilization for the promotion of religion, agriculture, and commerce," which he hoped would eclipse the slave trade he so abhorred.[36] Yet Livingstone unwittingly helped to open up the continent to exploitation of its human and natural resources by persons with less noble aspirations.

## Albert Schweitzer

Of all the missionaries to live and work in Africa, none is better known than Albert Schweitzer. He had earned doctorates in philosophy, theology, music and medicine by the time of his departure for Equatorial Africa (now known as Gabon).

In the role of physician, Schweitzer served there with a nondenominational group, the Paris Evangelical Missions. He labored at the forest hospital at Lambarene to bring good health to those he considered to be the neediest of the needy.

Schweitzer was not without his shortcomings, and some people have criticized his methods as overly paternalistic.[37] Yet few would find fault with his kindhearted and humble personality. Karl Reiland, in the introduction to *The Forest Hospital at Lambarene*, says of Schweitzer: "He has none of the self-consciousness that so often disfigures the manner of the artist, none of the intellectual conceit that is often met with in the celebrated scholar; no impatience, loftiness, or erudite reserve. Albert Schweitzer reminds me how 'Jesus took a towel and washed the disciples' feet.'"[38]

Schweitzer's attitude of kindness extended to all living creatures, in the tradition of St. Francis. The notion of "reverence for life" formed the cornerstone of his ethics. He maintains, "The first spiritual act in man's experience is reverence for life. The consequence of it is that he comes to realize his dependence on events quite beyond his control."[39] Elsewhere he writes, "Events cannot be harmonized with our activities. . . . We like to imagine that Man is nature's goal; but the facts do not support that belief."[40] For Schweitzer, humility goes beyond relations between humans to include human relations with the environment. He states:

> The great fault of all ethics hitherto has been that they believed themselves to deal only with the relations of man to man. In reality, however, the question is what is his attitude to the world and all life that come within his reach. A man is ethical only when Life, as such, is sacred to him, that of plants and animals as that of his fellow men; and devotes himself helpfully to all life that is in need of help.[41]

Schweitzer's book *The Forest Hospital at Lambarene* gives an account of how he demonstrated reverence for life in his work in Africa. He describes how he removed living creatures to safe locations and explained to observers his reason for doing so while he was laboring with Africans to clear a relocation site for the hospital. Of the Africans' reaction Schweitzer says, "Some smile in embarrassment; others pay no attention at all to what they have heard so often."[42] However, one day his patience finally was rewarded when an African related to a fellow worker and to a listening group "the theory that the animals were, like ourselves, created by God, and that he will some day hold a great palaver with the men who torment or kill them. This savage was the very last on whom I should have expected my deeds and words to make any impression."[43]

Teaching the Africans to extend their understanding of God's positive valuation of life to include plants was more problematical for Schweitzer. In clearing the site for the new hospital, he asked workers to transplant all the palm trees—a plant species that was, in Schweitzer's estimation, "value-less." He related, "That one should feel compassion for the animals my natives can understand. But that I should expect them to carry heavy palm trees about, so that they may live instead of being cut down, seems to them a perverted philosophy."[44]

Schweitzer apparently believed that his friends among the Belgian colonialists would regard his love for trees as did the Africans. The Belgians had been logging in the region for thirty years by the time Schweitzer arrived in the forest of Lambarene in 1913, and the missionary did not worry overly much about this activity, acknowledging to his wife that he was a "timber-fanatic."[45] He reasoned that just the trees near the river were affected by the logging, and he scoffed that "only . . . those who do not know what a forest in Equatorial Africa is like" would entertain the possibility of having a railroad into the interior. "In these forests," he reflected, "one learns how impotent Man is when pitted against Nature."[46]

Unfortunately, Schweitzer grossly underestimated the long-range need for protecting the natural environment from the impact of human civilization. In 1978, sixty-five years after Schweitzer's arrival in Lambarene, the first section (seventy miles) of the Trans-Gabon railroad was opened. Today much of Africa's interior land is abused.

## A Man of God?

One dramatic example of adverse missionary impact on the African environment is recorded by Colin Turnbull, an anthropologist. In a chapter from *The Lonely African* entitled "The Man of God," Turnbull tells the story of an early twentieth-century missionary, the Reverend Henry Spence, who went to the Belgian Congo, now Zaire. Turnbull is unclear about the source of this biographical sketch, though apparently the story of the missionary was told to him by an African whose bias against the man may result in some exaggeration. Turnbull asserts that the sketches in *The Lonely African*, however, tell basically factual narratives about real people, though the names and exact locations have been changed (see 123, 243-44). The account unfolds as follows, in the first-person voice of Spence:

> Shortly after crossing into the Congo we entered the forest, and for the first time I felt real fear. It was not fear of the savages, for I had no cause to worry about my bodily safety. I had committed myself in trust to the Lord, and He would look after me. I felt fear for another reason, fear for the people who lived in the forest, fear of the immensity of the task I had undertaken. For the forest was evil. I felt it as soon as I saw it, stretching away into the distance, far out of sight. As we drove down from the hills it closed in above us and I could sense the presence of evil all around. It was even on the faces of the natives as they came to stare at us from the roadside. It was everywhere. [47]

Spence continues,

I made up my mind that I would make it my work to bring the heathen out of the forest, to give them sunlight, to show them how to live in God's open world, to teach them to abandon this darkness, and I took courage from my resolution and gloried in God each time we came to a clearing where I could see the sky and the sun.[48]

The missionary resolved to expand the mission-school compound to which he had been assigned. His plan was for a modern school, unlike the existing one whose buildings "looked exactly like the native huts."[49] Spence describes the scene thus: "It was wonderful to see the forest coming down on all sides. I could feel the power of Satan receding as every tree fell. In a matter of months we had about ten acres cleared completely, and God's sunshine lit on the land for the first time."[50] An assistant by the name of Amboko resisted the missionary's zealous efforts. As Spence recounts it,

Amboko . . . put up an objection to almost every plan I made. He did not even like the cutting down of the forest, he said it would bring misfortune, unless we were going to use the ground for plantations. But I wanted the plantations to be outside the mission compound. He said that we should leave some trees standing for shade, and for the protection of the soil, and I suppose he was right, but I just felt that I wanted every tree down."[51]

Later, Amboko began to distance himself from Spence because of the latter's paternalistic, dogmatic attitude toward the traditional culture. His refusal to answer Spence's query as to why the Africans did not respect Spence and would not listen to the Word of God caused the missionary to be "suddenly filled with a dreadful loathing for him. . . . It was as though the forest had suddenly grown right back over my life, and was crushing me beneath it."[52] Turnbull's account gives no indication that Spence ever comprehended why Amboko came in time to renounce the Christian faith.

## William Carey

On the continent of Asia, the pioneering missionary efforts of William Carey—father of the modern missionary movement—are familiar to students of missions history. Few are aware, however, that Carey was distinguished as an amateur botanist (exemplified by his membership in the Linnaean Society and his founding of the Agricultural and Horticultural Society of India). His concern for the well-being of the total person ran deep. Carey planned from the beginning to raise food while he did his other work, which focused on education and biblical translation. His biographers commented on Carey's motivation as a missionary earthkeeper:

> He wanted to help [the Indians] to a life more abundant. We should have realized that his garden was never just an indulgence of a fascinating hobby, but an integral part of his missionary career, another proclamation of the philanthropy of God. His horticulture, like his preaching and his translation work, had one and the same motive, to enrich men with life's best. . . . Had Carey gone to India simply to follow the pursuits of a naturalist and not as a missionary of Jesus Christ, in all probability the very men who sneered would have been the first to extol.[53]

In 1811 Carey wrote a detailed paper on "the state of agriculture in Bengal, dealing with the various forms of grains and plants useful for commerce, . . . with suggestions for improved methods of cultivation." In that paper, he made an unprecedented call for the conservation of forests and for the introduction of new tree varieties.[54] Carey's call has largely gone unheeded; not only in South Asia but around the world, forests have been and continue to be decimated. Humankind now has the capacity for transforming the tropical rain forests into unproductive land as early as the year 2010.[55]

## Toyohiko Kagawa

In the nearly 200 years since Carey's initiation of the modern missionary movement, the church's understanding of mission has matured greatly. One case of missionary influence blossoming in the life of a national Christian was that of Toyohiko Kagawa, who came to the United States and witnessed here to his own vision of the Christian life. Kagawa, a remarkable Christian whose faith was nurtured by the Presbyterian missionary Harry Myers, devoted himself to a ministry characterized by both evangelism and social action. He became a powerful force for change in agriculture and other land issues, seeking out political involvements in which Myers, as an expatriate missionary, could not have engaged prudently.[56]

Following a period of urban ministry and labor organizing, Kagawa turned his attention to the peasant farmers of the countryside—many still victimized by a feudal landholding system, others struggling to make a living on tiny plots of land. As a key organizer of the peasant farmers' movement, Kagawa participated in elections on behalf of peasant interests and promoted laws to protect the peasants from abuse by landowners. Kagawa helped to organize the first peasant union in the country, started a magazine entitled *The Soil and Freedom* together with some of his associates, and worked toward land reform.[57] Following the disastrous earthquake in Tokyo in 1923, food scarcity led to the Japanese government's passing of Kagawa's Anti-Exploitation Land Act. This law gave the government power to confiscate any land being held by private interests for speculative purposes in order then to put such land to more productive use.[58]

Kagawa and his supporters had two aspects to their plan for improving the life of the farmers: introducing new crops and methods into the agricultural system, and forming farmer cooperatives. For several years, Kagawa traveled around the country teaching the farmers about Jesus and about what he called "biblical agriculture." Reflecting on the reference in Genesis to the "tree of life," Kagawa drew from J. Russell Smith's classic work, *Tree Crops: A Permanent Agriculture*, to envision planting trees on mountain slopes unsuitable for row crops.[59]

The "second lesson of biblical agriculture" for Kagawa is that Abel's pastoral way is better than Cain's agrarian approach where tillable land is at a premium, since goats can turn the weeds on mountainsides into milk. He describes other scriptural lessons as follows:

> Also in the Bible we find stories of soil selection, selection of seeds, and the method of pruning by Jesus. And we read in the eleventh chapter of Romans concerning the grafting of trees, and in the Old Testament how King Hezekiah restored desert land by putting in many kinds of trees. So in Japan we started to learn how to change our desert land into fertile land by reading the Bible.[60]

Not only through his words but above all through the example of his life-style, Kagawa taught what it means to have every aspect of one's life transformed by the spirit of Jesus. Referred to by his friends as a "modern St. Francis of Assisi,"[61] Kagawa reluctantly left the small hut where his family had lived for years in the slums of Kobe and, for the sake of his children, moved to a Tokyo suburb. He built a small house there out of scrap lumber, furnished mainly with crates. Kagawa believed that "if one lives a life of this sort near to a pool encircled by friendly trees, and fellowships daily with the owls and baby foxes, the intolerable city with its multitudinous noises loses its lure."[62]

## Educating for Missionary Earthkeeping

Kagawa's witness to modern exploitation of both natural and human resources challenges Christians everywhere to respond decisively to such abuse. This response requires spiritual, mental, and physical preparation if the earthkeeper is to serve God with heart, head, and hands. In an increasingly complex and specialized world, an effective Christian earthkeeper must be able to function competently in an interdisciplinary setting. The following viewpoints from professionals in higher education, cutting across disciplinary lines, address issues of education and preparation for responsible cross-cultural care of the earth.

### *Asian Theologians*

In the spring of 1977, The Occasional (now International) Bulletin of Missionary Research reported on a consultation entitled "Theological education for Christian Ministry in Asia" and attended by one hundred Asian theologians. A summary statement from one conference workshop examines the perspectives of Asian religions and culture on the relationship between humanity and the rest of creation, then looks at the ecological crisis and at biblical views of creation. The Asian theologians note an overemphasis in Christian tradition on God's transcendence and on human dominion over the nonhuman created order. Their statement concludes with several implications for theological education, the following of which are particularly pertinent to missionary preparation:

[1] Theological reflections on [humanity] and nature in Asia can meaningfully take place only in an interdisciplinary way.
[2] Theological students must be exposed directly to

ecological issues and to the problems caused by abso-
lutizing modernization and technology.
[3] The practice of training students merely to be ministers
in church-oriented situations must give way to broad-based
training for a variety of ministries. Included in this multi-
plicity of ministries is the ministry related to problems of
ecology.
[4] In some seminaries there is already an attempt to relate
theology to life in nature by the inclusion of agriculture in
the curriculum. This is to be encouraged.[63]

Regarding the last point, I would add that not only courses
in agriculture but also in ecology and environmental ethics
have begun to be included in seminary curricula, and more
courses in these areas are vital to the training of Christian
earthkeepers.

## *Luther Copeland*

Luther Copeland, a theological educator and missiologist
who spent much of his career in Asia, exhibits the ecological
sensitivity called for by these Asian theologians. A recent
book by this emeritus Southern Baptist missionary to Japan
is entitled *World Mission, World Survival: The Challenge and
Urgency of Global Missions Today.*[64] In a chapter called "Can
We Achieve a Livable World? World Mission and Survival
Issues," Copeland details five critical issues for human
survival: 1) war/peace, 2) poverty/hunger, 3) justice /human
rights, 4) priestly care of the environment, and 5) interreli-
gious relationships.

In his analysis of Christian responsibility toward God's
creation, Copeland moves beyond both dominion and
stewardship images when he asserts,

I believe that we human beings are called to be God's
priests in relation to the natural world. This meaning may
well be included in God's designation of Israel as a "king-
dom of priests" (Exod 19:6), a title which the church

inherited (1 Pet 2:9). The context is God's possession of "all
the earth" as well as "all peoples." . . . We are stewards,
but we are more than stewards. The connotation of stewardship may be too mechanical and managerial to express
our role adequately. We are priests who view the world
with reverence because it is God's handiwork. We are to
represent the creation to God and act toward it according
to [God's] attitude and intent.[65]

## C. Dean Freudenberger

One theological educator who, like Copeland, insists on
the necessity for an environmental dimension to the Christian
mission is C. Dean Freudenberger, currently professor of
international development and world missions at Claremont
School of Theology. This agronomist and ethicist has spoken
and written at length on the critical need for environmentally
sound approaches to agriculture. Freudenberger draws on a
wealth of experience as a Methodist missionary in Zaire, an
agricultural program officer for the World Division of the
United Methodist General Board of Global ministries, and a
trainer for Peace Corps volunteers in thirteen French-
speaking countries. His call for an ecologically sustainable
agriculture needs to be heard by any agricultural missionary
who aspires to serve as an earthkeeper.

In his 1984 book *Food for Tomorrow?* Freudenberger begins
by discussing the world food crisis, describing current stres-
ses on the world ecosystem and covering "land use, soil loss,
water and air pollution, and political and economic realities."
The second section of the book examines Old and New Testament sources for constructing "a new agricultural ethic
based on the guidelines of justice, participation, and sustainability."[66]

The third section explores some specific solutions to
agricultural problems both in the U.S. and overseas, and then
outlines the tasks of the church regarding environmentally
sound food production. The three areas of research and

experimentation that Freudenberger surveys are forest farming, herbaceous perennial polycultures (grasses and shrubs), and indigenous livestock. Each of these solutions has great potential application for missionary earthkeepers.

In his discussion of agroforestry, Freudenberger draws on the experience of Sholto Douglas and Robert Hart as reported in their book *Forest Farming: Towards a Solution to Problems of World Hunger and Conservation.*[67] The advantages of agroforestry are the tremendous yields per acre of certain tree crops relative to row crops, the ecological roles that trees play, and their compatibility with animal husbandry.[68]

Freudenberger comments that forest farming offers "one complete and integrated applied science instead of the conventional separation of silviculture from agriculture, a cleavage which is unknown to nature." Since overspecialization in agriculture and the predominance of monocultural approaches have done great damage by upsetting the ecological balance in many areas, integrated tree cropping could provide a creative alternate method of food production, especially in marginal lands not suitable to conventional farming methods.[69]

In a closing chapter entitled "The Tasks of the Church," Freudenberger asks whether the history of agriculture can be reversed. He asserts that such a reversal would first require "a shift from relating to the sustaining resources of the created world as objects for exploitation to seeing the resources of the earth as subjects of God's orderly creation and purpose." In the view of this former missionary agriculturist, "The problem of agriculture, domestic or international, is a profoundly spiritual matter. Working for the solution is a fundamental responsibility of the churches."[70]

## Earthkeeping in a Hungry World

The missionary agriculturist sent out from the United States more likely than not has received formal training in a

land-grant university. Formally trained agricultural missionaries, along with the more traditionally accepted medical
missionaries, have been the focus of attention in recent years
as the church has struggled with the physical hunger of
growing numbers of people in the face of droughts, wars,
and other calamities.

In 1978, an informal consultation entitled "Justice, the
Church, and the Land-Grant University" was convened at
Iowa State University, cosponsored by the university and the
(former) United Presbyterian Church in the USA, to explore
the roles of the church and the land-grant universities in
meeting the challenge of world hunger. The edited proceedings of this meeting have been published under the title *The
Agricultural Mission of Churches and Land-Grant Universities*. In
his presentation at this conference, William Gibson asserted
that the world hunger problem may stimulate both the
church and the land-grant universities to a renewed commitment to justice, a commitment common to the foundation of
both institutions but eroded over the years.[71]

Gibson, who is coordinator of the Eco-Justice Project at
the Centre for Religion, Ethics and Social Policy (Cornell
University, Ithaca, New York), discusses ways in which the
church and the land-grant university can be of mutual benefit
to each other: "Church and university need each other's
criticisms, as the university helps the church to relate its
ideals and visions to factual data and scientific insights into
social process, and the church reminds the university of the
moral responsibility to apply knowledge to the common
good."[72] Gibson says that "the church looks to the university
now for a holistic approach to world food issues, within
which there would be at least these major focuses: (1) Food
self-sufficiency for the poor . . . (2) Appropriate agricultural
technology . . . (3) Ecologically sustainable farming methods."[73] Regarding this last point, the church in its earthkeeping function may have to remind the university of its
moral responsibility both to pursue and apply knowledge in

the area of environmental conservation. According to Don Hadwiger, another participant at the conference, until recent years "the research establishment has been less than eager to anticipate resource scarcities . . . [and] has usually ignored environmental costs."[74]

An American-trained agriculturist, Uzo Igbozurike of Nigeria, sounds a note of warning about the export of capital- and technology-intensive agricultural practices to other nations. In his book *Agriculture at the Crossroads: A Comment on Agricultural Ecology*, Igbozurike points out the irony that "the more 'developed' agriculture becomes, the more alienated it is from its ecosystem and the more massive the total energy and environmental costs involved in food production."[75] He quotes the ecologist H. T. Odum as saying, "What a sad joke that a man from an industrial agricultural region goes to an underdeveloped country to advise on improving agriculture." Then Igbozurike comments, "The saddest part of the joke, of course, is that this itinerant does not just go; he is given a red-carpet gilt-edged invitation, and usually his pronouncements are accorded the unquestioned deference of a divine injunction."[76] Such deference is even more likely in the case of the missionary agriculturist who, whether intended or not, often speaks and acts with an aura of divine authority.

## The Vocation of Earthkeeping

Paul Brand has dedicated his career as a medical missionary chiefly to the care and treatment of persons with devastating diseases affecting the skin. In the last few years, Brand has devoted considerable attention to ecological problems. At the 1984 Au Sable Forum he offered a firsthand perspective on deforestation in India, where he lived as a child and later served as a missionary. "I would gladly give up medicine tomorrow if by so doing I could have some influence on policy with regard to mud and soil. The world will die from lack of pure water and soil long before it will die from a lack of antibiotics or surgical skill and knowledge."[77] Were Brand a young man today faced with career options, he might well choose missionary earthkeeping. In Luther Copeland's view,

> Earthkeeping now should be seen as an essential part of the Christian mission. There is a call for Christians who will give themselves specifically to this vocation and for some to fulfill this calling as cross-cultural missionaries. The larger summons is for all of us to support this aspect of the Christian mission and to contribute to it according to our abilities.[78]

Prospective vocational missionary earthkeepers, and missions administrators as well, will be more likely to sense the Spirit moving in the direction of environmental responsibility if more Christians join their voices with Copeland's in sounding this call.

Looking back, I realize that my educational goals were shaped by time spent on my grandparents' farm—or, rather, not on the farm per se, but a thirty-acre forest on the farm that in recent years has been designated a natural heritage area by the state of Tennessee. This old-growth white pine and hemlock forest is one of the few remaining examples of the land cover that gave the surrounding area the name "Shady Valley."

My grandmother gets the credit for protecting these woods from family members and outsiders alike who suggested from time to time that the trees ought to be cut. The forest even prevailed during the Great Depression, when the farm was providing for the needs of a family of nine as well as frequent guests. The words of Wendell Berry, a farmer-poet and leading proponent of sustainable agriculture, conveys a lesson that I learned on this farm:

> An enduring agriculture must never cease to consider and respect and preserve wildness. The farm can exist only

within the wilderness of mystery and natural force. And if the farm is to last and remain in health, the wilderness must survive within the farm. That is what agricultural fertility is: the survival of the natural process in the human order. . . .

The farm must yield a place to the forest, not as a wood lot, or even as a necessary agricultural principle, but as a sacred grove—a place where the Creation is let alone, to serve as instruction, example, refuge; a place for people to go, free of work and presumption, to let themselves alone.[79]

For me, this East Tennessee farm and forest have been a sanctuary where I have often contemplated and sought God's will for my life. Among those trees I considered the possibility and later concluded that God was calling me to use my skills in mission service overseas.

My first direct involvement in international mission inspired me to learn more about an ethical approach to resource management from a Christian, biblical perspective. But when I shared this sense of call with the missionary registrar of the seminary where I was then working (one of the leading theological schools in Africa), he replied that Christian interest in ecology during the early 1970s was a passing fad rather than a serious area of study. Though my own pilgrimage in missionary earthkeeping has continued in spite of this man's ill-informed advice, I have wondered how the church might find ways to insure that its leaders affirm vocational earthkeeping rather than deny or ignore its validity.

## The Church's Earthkeeping Task: Modeling, Educating, and Supporting

The focus of much of this chapter has been on individuals who, acting independently, have had an impact on the natural environment for better or for worse. But there is also a corporate role for the church today in educating, training, guiding, and supporting those who have experienced a special calling as missionaries. Part of that educating and guiding work involves embodying earthkeeping values in the policies, properties, and programs of the Church.

Slowly, mission strategies are beginning to reflect environmental concern. For example, the American Baptist Board of International Ministries now operates on the assumption that "the Christian mission is to the whole creation. We understand this to encompass not only the geographical dimension but also all the areas of life upon which the Christian gospel can be brought to bear."[80]

In this information age, education of clergy and laity alike regarding the earthkeeping commitments of denominations and other Christian organizations must be accomplished in part through print and other media. For example, World Vision inaugurated a quarterly publication in 1983 called *Together* that addresses issues of development, echoing common themes of the Missions Advanced Research and Communications Center and the Lausanne Committee for World Evangelization. This publication, which reflects the interdisciplinary, holistic approach of World Vision teams, included an editorial in an early issue entitled "Is There a Tree in Your Life?" The writer highlights "the need for awareness . . . of the inescapable importance of building trees and forestry into all of our integrated ministry."[81]

As our world becomes more urbanized and land is developed at an increasing pace, "sacred groves" fall prey to modern-day "missionaries of progress" and are rare indeed. The church quite properly has acquired land to be set aside as retreat or conference centers as well as church camps. When their development is compatible with the environment, as is the Au Sable Institute of Environmental Studies (Mancelona, Michigan), these auxiliary properties help to demonstrate Christian care of the Earth for all who visit.

Often these centers and camps are the setting for missions education programs. Christian educators have a golden opportunity to teach missionary earthkeeping through nature study and missions presentations. Ecologically sound gardening and agroforestry projects could become part of the activities for the children and youth.

Church administrators with responsibility for formal orientation or continuing education of cross-cultural missionaries and short-term overseas volunteers should seize this opportunity to sensitize missionaries to their potential environmental impact overseas. Familiarity with the local environment and natural history must be emphasized as an important part of on-the-field orientation.

Because of the quiet impact such church centers make on future missionaries and the entire church constituency who sojourn there, every effort should be made to create new retreat and conference centers (or modify existing ones) to promote environmental sensitivity. Renewable energy (solar, wind, or water power), soil and water conservation, recycling programs, low-impact transportation, and simple, healthy meals that reflect and explicitly teach sustainable food production should be incorporated into the holistic witness and ministry of these centers. Thus, Christians will be encouraged by their surroundings to examine their own life-styles and their relationship to the natural environment.

We are called to be priests to creation; ours is a ministry to all the Earth. This assertion may sound strange to the ears of some missions-minded Christians. But its acceptance simply involves an extension of the traditional missionary role of the physician and healer to include all of God's creation. As "patient," the Earth is in desperate need of healing. Richard St. Barbe Baker looked at the planet's trees like a skin, a protective covering. Anyone who loses more than one-third of his or her skin faces certain death.[82] Deforestation and the resulting soil erosion are stripping the skin off our planet. St. Barbe Baker took this problem so seriously that he gave his life to planting trees and organizing others to do so.

The task of missionary earthkeeping covers a broad range of fields and issues that extend beyond the scope of this study. Much research needs to be done in the area of missions history to explore further how and why missionaries kept (or failed to keep) the garden wherever they served. Yet because the need for protecting and conserving our natural environment has implications for every aspect of human life, we should not be limited by historical models of missionary earthkeeping, but rather should be inspired to discover ever new forms of "ministry to the earth."[83]

# Notes

[1]For an in-depth study of dark/black imagery in Western religious and secular thought, see Eulalio R. Baltazar, *The Dark Center: A Process Theology of Blackness* (New York: Paulist Press, 1973). A contemporary corollary is the term "Third World," now increasingly avoided in missionary and development circles because of the suggestion that the nonaligned or economically disadvantaged nations are less important or central in world affairs than the industrialized nations. The more descriptive term "two-thirds world" is often substituted.

[2]E. Luther Copeland, *World Mission, World Survival: The Challenge and Urgency of Global Missions Today* (Nashville: Broadman Press, 1985), 45–47.

[3]*Eerdmans' Handbook to the History of Christianity* (Grand Rapids: William. B. Eerdmans, 1977), 184.

[4]Count de Montalembert, *The Monks of the West*, 2 (Boston: Patrick Donahue, 1872), 190.

[5]Pope Saint Gregory the Great, *Life and Miracles of Benedict*, book two of the Zimmerman, O.S.B., and Benedict R. Avery, O.S.B. (Collegeville, MN: St. John's Abbey Press, 1949), 27–28.

[6](Middlesex, England: Penguin Books, 1964), 75.

[7]Clarence J. Glacken, *Traces on the Rhodian Shore* (Berkeley: University of California Press, 1961), 310.

[8]Saint Benedict, *The Rule of Saint Benedict*, trans. Cardinal Gasquet (New York: Cooper Square Publishers, 1966), 84.

[9]Glacken, 294. This work provides a wealth of information on the attitudes of medieval monks, which in turn influenced their management of the land.

[10]Ibid., 348.

[11]Christopher Dawson, *The Making of Europe: An Introduction to the History of European Unity*, cited by Glacken, *Traces on the Rhodian Shore*, 294.

[12]Robert K. Winter, *The Forest and Man*, 1st ed. (New York: Vantage Press, 1974), chap. 9, esp. 197–203.

[13]Norman F. Cantor, *Medieval History: The Life and Death of a Civilization* (New York: Macmillan, 1966), 190.

[14]Lowrie J. Daly, *Benedictine Monasticism: Its Formation and Development through the 12th Century* (New York: Sheed and Ward, 1965), 246.

[15]Cantor, *Medieval History*, 191.

[16]Carl A. Volz, *The Church of the Middle Ages: Growth and Change from 600 to 1400* (St. Louis: Concordia Publishing House, 1970), 59.

[17]*The Catholic Encyclopedia*, Universe ed. (London: Universal Knowledge Foundation), s.v. "Monasticism."

[18]Robert Kirby Winters, *The Forest and Man*, 1st ed. (New York: Vantage Press, 1974), 199.

[19](New York: Harper and Brothers, 1960), 209, 213.

[20]Winters, 201.

[21]Lynn White, Jr., "The Historical Roots of Our Ecological Crisis," *Science* 155 (March, 1967): 1205.

[22]Ibid.

[23]Ibid., 1206.

[24]Ibid., 1207.

[25]Ibid., 1208.

[26]Neill, *History of Christian Missions*, 116.

[27]Ibid.

[28]Copeland, *World Mission*, 47.

[29]René Dubos, *A God Within* (New York: Charles Scribner's Sons, 1972), 168.

[30]Ibid., 45.

[31]Ibid., 168.

[32]Copeland, *World Mission*, 47.

[33]See H. Paul Santmire, *The Travail of Nature: The Ambiguous Ecological Promise of Christian Theology* (Philadelphia: Fortress Press, 1985), 117–18 for further assessment of the Francis /Benedict discussion by Dubos.

[34]Neill, *History of Christian Missions*, 66.

[35](Englewood Cliffs: Prentice-Hall, Inc., 1980), 65.

[36]Ibid., 64.

[37]*Eerdmans' Handbook*, 596.

[38]Albert Schweitzer, *The Forest Hospital at Lambarene*, intro. by Karl Reiland (New York: Henry Holt, 1931), 8–9.

[39]Albert Schweitzer, "The Ethics of Reverence for Life," *Christendom*, 1, no. 2 (Chicago: Willet, Clark, 1936), in *Reverence for Life*, ed. Thomas Kiernan (New York: Philosophical Library, 1963), 48.

[40]Ibid., 42.

[41]Albert Schweitzer, *Out of My Life and Thought*, trans. C. T. Champion (New York: Holt, Reinhart, and Winston, 1963), 48.

[42]Schweitzer, *Forest Hospital*, 171.

[43]Ibid., 170.

[44]Ibid., 175.

[45]Ibid., 110.

[46]Ibid., 95.

[47](New York: Simon and Schuster, 1962), 109–110.

[48]Ibid.

[49]Ibid.

[50]Ibid., 114–115.

[51]Ibid., 119.

[52]Ibid.

[53]Pearce Carey, *William Carey* (London: Carey Press, 1942), 115.

[54]Ibid., 185.

[55]"Deforestation: The Human Costs," *Cultural Survival Quarterly* 6 (Spring 1982): 3.

[56]Charles R. Erdman, "Toyohiko Kagawa: A Tribute," *Princeton Seminary Bulletin* 52 (October 1958): 27–29.

[57]Emerson O. Bradshaw, *Unconquerable Kagawa* (St. Paul: Macalestar Park Publishing, 1952), 99.

[58]Ibid., 111.

[59]Ibid., 100; Freudenberger, *Food for Tomorrow?*, 116. Among the 100-plus books produced by Kagawa is a Japanese translation of Smith's

*The World's Food Resources.* See the biographical sketch of him by Elanor M. Hinder and Helen F. Topping in Kagawa's *Love, the Law of Life,* trans. J. Fullerton Gressitt (Chicago: John C. Winston, 1929).

⁶⁰Ibid., 101.

⁶¹Erdman, "Totohiko Kagawa," 29.

⁶²William Axling, *Kagawa,* 11th ed. (New York: Harper & Brothers, 1932), 148.

⁶³Ibid., 148-49.

⁶⁴"Man and Nature: Workshop Statement by Asian Theologians," *Occasional Bulletin of Missionary Research* 1 (April 1977): 21.

⁶⁵Copeland, *World Mission,* 122.

⁶⁶C. Dean Freudenberger, *Food for Tomorrow?* (Minneapolis: Augsburg Publishing House, 1984), 9.

⁶⁷Rev. ed. (London: Watkins, 1980).

⁶⁸Freudenberger, 114–19.

⁶⁹Ibid., 119-20.

⁷⁰Ibid., 145.

⁷¹Dieter T. Hessel, ed. (Ames, IA: The Iowa State University Press, 1980), 14–15.

⁷²Ibid., 18.

⁷³Ibid., 16–18.

⁷⁴Ibid., 18.

⁷⁵(Ile-Ife, Nigeria: University of Ife Press, n.d. [197?]), 20.

⁷⁶Ibid., 83.

[77]Paul Brand, "A Handful of Mud." Originally presented at the Au Sable Forum on the Theology of Creation, Au Sable Institute of Environmental Studies, 1984 and published in the proceedings of this forum, it was subsequently published in *Christianity Today* (19 April, 1985), 26–27 and in *Tending the Garden*, ed. Wesley Granberg-Michaelson (1987), 136–50.

[78]Copeland, *World Mission*, 123.

[79]*The Unsettling of America: Culture and Agriculture* (New York: Avon Books, 1977), 130–31.

[80]Dean R. Kirkwood, ed., *Seeing Missions Today: An Overview of American Baptist Overseas Missions* (Valley Forge: International Ministries, ABD, 1984), 50.

[81]W. Dayton Roberts, *Together* 4 (July-Sept 1984): 4.

[82]"The Skin of the Earth," *Warm Wind* (Spring 1980): 16, cited in Freudenberger, *Food for Tomorrow?*, 115.

[83]This is the title of a course taught at Claremont School of Theology by C. Dean Freudenberger.

# Chapter 2

# The Ecological Awareness of the Amazon Indians

## by Ghillean T. Prance

At the time of the discovery of America, American Indians were profoundly religious and mystical human beings. A great part of their daily existence was bound in religious rites, in propitiating their many gods, in finding grace, justification and peace. Every act had its religious significance, every wind, every change in color of the moon, every appearance of the unexpected, had its religious portent. In such highly developed cultures as the Aztec and Inca, a large priesthood served to interpret the will of the gods. A mystical philosophy, a questioning of the essence of human existence, informed and disciplined the attitude of the Indian toward life and death.[1]

What is still far from clear, four centuries later, is how deep was the conversion to Christianity. Mass movements carried forward by political and cultural factors rarely produces [sic] pure forms of religions. For most Indians the addition of another deity to their polytheistic world was not greatly disturbing. In many Indian villages today it is difficult to discern whether there has been a genuine Christian baptism of the ancient religious cults, or whether the old beliefs remain, covered only by a veneer of Christian practice and always ready to break through when needed.[2]

The quotations above illustrate some of the problems of missionary work among indigenous peoples, especially when the missionary is aware of environmental issues and the full extent of the biblical teaching on creation. The more we can understand an indigenous culture and the deeper our understanding of biblical teachings on the stewardship of creation, the more firm a Christian belief we can bring to the tribal people. Without a deep understanding of the culture in which we are working, it is easy to bring North American and European culture rather than, or as well as, a true faith. It is essential to work out for oneself what the basic requirements are for a true belief in Christ and to separate them from those additional practices to which we have become accustomed because they are part of our culture.

One example of acculterated habits is the insistence of many missionaries to settle semi-nomadic, cultivating Indians around a central mission station where a traditional church building can be built. This settlement completely disrupts much of the sound ecological practices in which the tribe is engaged and later leads to many problems, such as their inability to sustain themselves as soil becomes impoverished and game decreases. The Bible does not insist upon such a cultural practice; in fact, the house churches that would be more suitable for this type of Indian life were apparently common practice in the times of the early Church. This volume demonstrates that second-generation missionaries can develop a deep cultural understanding that enables them also to become concerned earthkeepers.[3]

One of the great privileges of my job as a botanical explorer and a Christian is to have had the opportunity to visit many different mission works. I have been hosted by Bible translators in remote tribes, flown by Missionary Aviation Fellowship planes, and also have had the opportunity to speak in large urban churches in cities such as São Paulo. This travel has allowed me to get to know the mission field well. In the process I have seen good and bad mission work, sensitive and insensitive. The things that I would call bad, or ecologically unsound, however, are generally done in complete innocence rather than from any bad intentions. The overemphasis on conversion without calculating its results on the life of the converts can lead to many misunderstandings. The purpose of this chapter is not to criticize mission work, but to call Christians (and especially mission candidates) to include the ecological imperatives of Scripture in their theology. Schools that are training missionary candidates must give them the theological basis that will make them ecologically aware and culturally sensitive.

The ecological awareness and respect for creation that I have observed in the Indians of the Latin American region does not mean that I accept an ultimate pluralism of religious values. I do not, for example, condone native beliefs such as animism or worship of objects of creation rather than the Creator. Anyone who has traveled among the Indians can see the good points that I will emphasize with regard to ecological awareness and at the same time note the evil in their lives, often expressed in fighting, raids, poisoning, and so forth. Thus, the effort here is not to portray French philosopher Jean Jacques Rousseau's concept of the noble savage, for all have sinned and come short of the glory of God. A realization of the ecology of indigenous peoples and of their reverence for nature, however, can lead to the establishment of a much more permanent and environmentally sound Christian faith based on the similar respect for nature that we find in the Bible. What we should seek to avoid is the example of mission work found in Siberut:

> The manner in which Christianity has been brought to Siberut has had a devastating effect on the island. The traditional religion with its complex set of taboos against the exploitation of nature is now replaced by a bold form of Christianity with no feeling of stewardship, and which ignores the reasons for which traditional beliefs evolved. This has led to a basic change in the economy of the island,

with considerably strong emphasis on producing surplus for sale, clearing more land, gathering more rattan, wearing store-bought cloth, growing the "more civilized" rice rather than sago and settling down close to a church.[4]

All environmentally aware Christians who have traveled the mission field can think of similar examples of poor ecological stewardship; Mutombo Mpanya's essay in this volume is a good example from Zaire. I think of the nutritional deficiencies caused among a group of Kayapo Indians in Brazil when a missionary persuaded them to abandon the small and inferior-looking varieties of cassava in favor of huge, attractive-looking ones from the nearby town. The difference was that the new variety contained virtually no protein. The small amounts of vital amino acids in the traditional varieties were crucial to the nutrition of the tribe. The problem is that frequently such changes are made by missionaries with the best of intentions but without adequate consideration or knowledge of environmental factors. The preceding example illustrates the need for education of missionary candidates in both ecological and theological matters.

## Indian Examples

### *Guarana and Its Ants*

Many tropical plants have an amazing protection against insect predators through the use of another insect as its protector. Often the friendly insect is attracted to the plant by sugar-producing, extrafloral nectaries. There are many species of ants that feed from these nectaries and at the same time ward off leaf-eating insects. One such plant with leaf-nectaries is the guarana, long cultivated by the Maues and other Indian groups for use as a stimulant, since the fruits are more caffeine-rich than coffee beans. The famous German explorer Alexander von Humboldt first described this species after finding it in use by Indians in Venezuela. Few people have noticed that the young leaves of this plant have little "knobs" at the vein endings around their margins. These are nectaries that secrete sugar and feed the ants. As the leaves mature, becoming hard and unappetizing to leaf-eating insects, the nectaries disappear and cannot be seen. I was amazed when a Maues Indian with whom I was walking picked up part of an ant colony and moved it from one patch of guarana plants to another, explaining that the plants grew better with the friendly ants present. This type of protection granted by extrafloral nectaries has only recently been worked out by biologists, yet the Indians have been using it as an aid in their cultivation of guarana for centuries! They also have many legends about guarana and its origins that contribute to their respect and conservation of the species.

## The Chacobo Indians of Bolivia: The Use of Wild Species

Conservationists and people in search of new useful plants have long said that the Amazon Indians have a multitude of uses for the forest. One of my postdoctoral scientists, Brian M. Boom, recently made a study of the Chacobo Indians of Bolivia. He made a forest inventory of a hectare (two and one-half acres) of forest in Chacobo territory where every tree was collected and identified as to species. His results showed that the Indians had a use for eighty-two percent of the species of trees (seventy-five of the ninety-one species) representing ninety-five percent of the individual trees (619 of the 649 trees) in the stand. Uses included such things as medicines, edible fruits, fuel, craft and building materials. Fourteen species were used as a fuel for cooking and for smoking rubber to coagulate the latex; thirty-three provided edible fruit; twenty-three were used in crafts and construction; and another twenty-three were used for medicinal purposes by the Chacobo. In addition to the trees quantified in this study, the Chacobo had uses for many other plants in the shrub and herb layer of the forest. This use of the tropical forest diversity and their understanding of so many of the plants is what enables the forest Indians to live well in an environment that Westerners have found hard to manage.[5] Missionaries have often sought to replace this type of diversity life-style with an agricultural system that depends upon a single crop!

## Indian Agroforestry: The Cultivation of Species

Agroforestry—the mixed cropping of trees and herbaceous crops as a diverse ecosystem—is a comparatively recent term to foresters and agriculturalists alike. In practice, however, it is an old concept that has been and is being used by indigenous populations around the world. Formerly cultivated fields that are no longer actively cultivated by shifting cultivators have usually been identified as abandoned or fallow. There is an increasing literature showing that this is not abandonment, but the encouragement of a managed system of regeneration that simulates the natural process and allows the inclusion of a greater number of potentially useful species. For example, such processes have been reported in Zaire, Africa by Dubois (1979), in New Guinea by Clarke (1971) and Hyndman (1982), in Micronesia by Yen (1974), in Mexico by Alcorn (1984), in South America among the Bora Indians of Peru by Denevan et al. (1984), and among the Yanomamo of Brazil by Prance (1984). Any of these examples would demonstrate a deep understanding of the management of agriculture and forestry in rainforest areas that is infinitely superior to most of the monoculture systems imposed on the region by Western influence.

The case of the Bora Indians of Peru (Denevan et al. 1984) is one with which I am familiar. The Bora are typical swidden cultivators who cut and burn patches of primary forest or at least twenty-year-old secondary forest for their short-term fields to grow such crops as corn, rice, cow peas, or cassava. Even their primary fields are a lesson in ecology because they are a mosaic of different interspersed crops rather than pure stands of one. This makes it harder for insect pests to find any individual crop because it is hidden in patches among the other crops. The Indian practice is to use this land for one or two plantings only of primary crops such as cassava. Even within crops there is considerable diversity. The Bora Indians, for instance, plant twenty-two varieties of cassava. They realize that the soil becomes too poor to sustain further short-term plantings and so allow the gradual conversion of the land from a short-term cropping system to a long-term agroforestry system.

The change to an agroforestry system is done by planting various useful trees such as the fruit, umari (*Poraqueiba sericea*), and leaving a few trees from the original forest (tropical cedar, *Cedrela odorata*), while others such as copal (*Hymenaea courbaril*) resprout from coppice shoots on stumps of old primary forest trees. By the time the fallow was nineteen years old, a total of eighty-two species of trees were counted on the fallows studied by Denevan and others (1984), twenty-two of which had well-defined uses.

One of the most interesting aspects of this regeneration is that the Bora closely follow what natural regeneration would be of an abandoned forest. Thus, early annual species of a natural succession are replaced by rice or corn; bananas replace Heliconia, a relative of the banana that is an important part of succession. The Bora plant bananas in low shady areas where Heliconia plants are common. Next they plant uvilla (*Pourouma cecropiifolia*), an important edible grape-like fruit that closely resembles its related genus, *Cecropia*, the most ubiquitous tree of secondary colonization. Their clustering of trees shows that they are aware of ecological difference caused by local topography: for example, some species are clustered on slopes, while others are on plane ground.

In the Bora study, 133 different useful species of plant were identified in their fallows. Through the use of fruits, nuts, and other edible products the Bora diet is significantly enhanced with the addition of a continuous variety of proteins, minerals, fats, and vitamins to the carbohydrate-rich products of their agriculture. In addition, the fallow also provides such products as condiments, construction material, drugs, tools, and crafts. The Bora thus appear to manage "abandoned" land excellently. Significantly, similar systems have been adopted by Peruvian settlers of nearby areas. Such a system in the village of Tamshiyacu provides cash crops such as the Brazil nut and umari fruit. The study of such indigenous models is likely to yield much more about agroforestry technique than we would know beginning research de novo. One of the secrets of Bora success is their use of biological diversity.

Missionaries, scientists, and other outsiders would do well to learn all about such systems before advocating any changes. Unfortunately, one outside influence that is changing the model system of the Bora is mission work! Yet, the Bora system shows that they have a deep knowledge of at least three important ecological processes: 1) soil depletion and enrichment; 2) secondary succession; and 3) biological diversity. Both the Chacobo and the Bora studies emphasize that the success of the Indians living in rainforest areas is due to their use of biological diversity. The first tendency of Westerners—whether developers or missionaries—is to try to simulate the corn fields of Iowa or the potato fields of Idaho where a single monoculture crop dominates. This approach will work in the temperate region where the missionaries grew up because of the cold winter that kills off pests each year. These Western systems are just not the best for the tropics, where pests abound, the soil is poor, and soil micro-rhizae are essential for the uptake of nutrients by the crops.

## The Kayapo Indians

The other Amazon Indian group that has been well studied ecologically is the Kayapo (see Posey 1982, 1983; Kerr

& Posey, 1984). Posey (1984) showed that the Kayapo are also involved in an agroforestry system similar to that of the Bora. In fact, study led Posey (1984) to term the old fields of the Gorotire Kayapo as "anything-but-abandoned fields" because of their extensive use of these ecosystems. For example, they have harvested bananas of some varieties for fifteen to twenty years after abandonment; anato (*Bixa*) for twenty-five years; and their unique source of carbohydrate flour, the cupa (*Cissus gongyloides*), for forty years.

The Kayapo, however, have many other interesting ecological practices, a few of which may be mentioned. Like many other Amazon tribes, they were accustomed to travel extensively through their vast territory between the Tocantico and Arajuaia rivers. Indians do not travel loaded with the heavy rucksacks that we tend to take on our expeditions. They cannot transport food for 150 to 200 people on their way to visit another village, and food gathering cannot be left solely to chance. Consequently, they bring useful food-yielding plants and plant them in spots along their trails and campsites. These "forest fields," as Posey termed them, make it easy for future travelers on the trail. Their plantings include botanical material to provide for the basic necessities of their life—food, medicinal plants, cleansing agents, hair and body oils, insect repellents, leaves for cooking, construction materials, and so forth. Some of these resources are concentrated into forest fields near their campsites, but others are planted along the Kayapo trails. They often clear a strip about twelve feet wide and plant the trail sides with such things as yams, sweet potatoes, and other tuber crops such as *Calathea*, a plant well adapted to grow in the low light of the forest. They also plant many medicinal plants and fruit trees along their trails. For the uninitiated, it may look very much like primary forest, but in fact the trail sides are highly managed and productive areas in which the Indians simulate the natural ecosystem and make a productive zone along the trails. Travel is easy when the whole trail is a supermarket.

The Kayapo also use natural or man-made openings in the forest as areas for gardens. These openings are caused either by natural fall of large trees from storms or where they have cut down a tree for some reason—such as to gather honey from a beehive in a tree. In these forest gaps, they replace the natural succession with such semidomesticated crops as manioc, taro, cupa, yams, sweet potatoes, or beans. They have noted that these crops thrive in such habitats and that productivity is greater than that for open-field plantations. This level of productivity probably occurs because fewer soil nutrients are lost. The Kayapo's use of the forest is significant for the development of the region because the same ecological principles need to be built into agroforestry programs.

The cupa is a vine, the stem of which yields a flour that is an important dietary item of the Kayapo. A taboo, however, forbids the young people to eat this source of carbohydrate. Cupa has a scaly stem resembling wrinkled skin. The Kayapo believe that eating cupa when young will cause one to become old. The social implication of this taboo is important, because it means that there is always adequate food for the old people![6]

The Brazil nut (*Bertholletia excelsa*) is the third-most-important fruit tree for the Kayapo, and they plant it in forest clearings exactly in accordance with the way it grows naturally: sprouting up in the light gap caused by a fuller tree. For the Kayapo, it is their favorite tree to plant for various family occasions, especially the birth of a first child. Near a Kayapo village, an Indian will often point to a Brazil nut tree in the forest and say "that tree was planted when my first child was born," or "the chief planted that tree when his daughter was married." This use of ceremonial planting gives the trees a value they would not otherwise have. Thus well protected, the trees can then provide the resources needed by the tribe.

# Conclusions

We do not want missionary work among indigenous peoples to turn out like that practiced among the Palikur Indians of Amapa Territory, Brazil, which was reported on by Arnaud (1980). The entire tribe converted to a form of Pentecostal Christianity after the work of several missionaries, including missionary linguistic experts. In this case, one of the mistakes made was turning the Indians from their hunter-gathering style of life to a market economy. They became dependent on working for the mission station and especially on other local people, who were ready to exploit them. The Indians frequently were quoted 2 Thessalonians 3:10b: "If anyone will not work, neither let him eat." This statement runs contrary to the Indians' sense of common property by which they share any game that they have hunted. Many times I have seen a hunter bring in a tapir or wild pig and divide it up among his fellow tribesmen who have spent the day at home, with the hunter keeping only a small piece to feed his own family!

To establish an Indian church, it is vital to understand the ecology of the Indians before attempting to make changes in their life-style. This will make both a significant contribution to our knowledge of the rainforest environment and ways in which it might be used, and also establish more permanent mission work that brings greater praise to our Lord. Indeed, as the Brazilian experience has shown, mission work in which ecology is not involved may result in the extinction of the people it has come to save. That result cannot possibly be a fulfillment of the great commission of Matthew 28:19.

The recent declaration of the "First Nations," made by North American Indians of Canada at the Assembly of First Nations Conference (Toronto, 1980), shows that these people know and respect the Creator. It reads

We the Original Peoples of this land know the Creator put us here.

The Creator gave us laws that govern all our relationships to live in harmony with nature and mankind.

The laws of the Creator defined our rights and responsibilities.

The Creator gave us our spiritual beliefs, our languages, our culture, and a place on mother earth which provided us with all our needs.

We have maintained our freedom, our languages, and our traditions from time immemorial.

We continue to exercise the rights and fulfill the responsibilities and obligations given to us by the Creator for the land upon which we were placed.

The Creator has given us the right to govern ourselves and the right to self-determination.

The rights and responsibilities given to us by the Creator cannot be altered or taken away by any other Nation.

We do not want to destroy this belief and respect for the Creator and for creation. We want to add to knowledge about the Creator as revealed through Christ Jesus. To do so, we must have a biblical theology that includes a fundamental respect for creation, as there is in Psalm 8:3-4. The Psalmist ponders the majesty of God's creation and is humbled by it:

When I look at thy heavens, the work of thy fingers,
the moon and the stars which thou has established;
What is man that thou art mindful of him,
and the son of man that thou dost care for him?

Yet at the same time the Psalmist speaks of responsibility for this creation in verse 6:

Thou hast given him dominion over the works of his hands;
thou has put all things under his feed, all sheep and oxen,
and also the beasts of the field, the birds of the airs, and

the fish of the sea, whatever passes along the paths of the sea.
0 Lord, our Lord, How majestic is thy name in all the earth.

The Christian who studies the depth of the biblical teachings about the care of creation will be concerned that the effects of evangelization and social projects be environmentally sound. In this way, disasters—like that described by Mutombo Mpanya in a village in Zaire—will be averted. To be effective for good, Christianity must include in its teachings a respect for nature that is equal to or exceeds that of the indigenous peoples of the world. In Job chapters 39 and 40, there are keen observations on nature, such as noting how the ostrich buries its egg, and an acknowledgment of God's control of nature. Moreover, the wisdom of Solomon was respected because "he spoke of trees, from the cedar that is in Lebanon even to the hyssop that grows on the wall; he spoke also of animals and birds and creeping things and fish. And men came from all peoples to hear the wisdom of Solomon."[7]

One writer of the Proverbs was obviously an astute student of animal behavior:

Four things are small on the earth,
But they are exceedingly wise:
The ants are not a strong folk;
But they prepare their food in summer;
The badgers are not a mighty folk,
Yet they make their homes in rocks:
The locusts have no king,
Yet all of them go out in ranks:
The lizard you may grasp with the hands,
Yet it is in the King's palaces.[8]

We would do well to listen to Job's advice to his comforters:

But now ask the beasts and let them teach you;
And the birds of the heavens, and let them tell you.

Or speak to the earth, and let it teach you;
And let the fish of the sea declare to you
Who among all these does not know
That the hand of the Lord has done this.[9]

This rich form of Christianity that understands creation as well as the Creator is what is needed in the mission field to avoid ecological disaster and to create a more stable and sustainable life system for those whom we seek to help.

# Bibliography

Alcorn, J. B. "Development Policy, Forests and Peasant Farms: Reflections on Huastec-managed Forests' Contributions to Commercial Production and Resource Conservation." *Economic Botany* 38 (1984): 389–406.

Arnaud, E. "0 Protestantismo entre os Indios Palikur do Rio Urucana (Oiapoque, Brasil)." *Revista Antropologia* 23 (1980): 99–102.

Beeson, T., and J. Pearce. *A Vision of Hope: The Churches and Change in Latin America*. Philadelphia: Fortress Press, 1984.

Boom, B. M. "Advocacy Botany for the Neotropics." *Garden* 9:3 (1985b): 24–32.

_____. "Amazon Indians and the Forest Environment." *Nature* 314 (1985a): 324.

Clarke, W. C. *Place and People: An Ecology of a New Guinean Community*. Berkeley: University of California Press, 1971.

Denevan, W. M., J. M. Treacy, J. B. Alcorn, et al. "Indigenous Agroforestry in the Peruvian Amazon: Bora Indian Management of Swidden Fallows." *Interciencia* 9 (1984): 346-56.

Dubois, J. "Aspects of Agroforestry Systems Used in Moyombe and Lower Congo (Zaire)." 84–90 in *Workshop: Agro-forestry Systems in Latin America*. Edited by G. de las Sala. Turrialba, Costa Rica: CATIE, 1979.

Hyndman, D. C. "Biotope Gradient in a Diversified New

Guinea Subsistence System." *Human Ecology* 10 (1982): 219–59.

Kerr, W. E., and D. A. Posey. "Informacioes Adicionais sobre a Agricultura dos Kayapo." *Interciencia* 9 (1984): 392–400.

Posey, D. A. "The Keepers of the Forest." *Garden* 6 (1982): 18–24.

# Notes

[1]Frank Tannenbaum, *Ten Keys to Latin America* (New York: Knopf, 1962), 53.

[2]Trevor Beeson and Jeremy Pearce, *A Vision of Hope: The Churches and Change in Latin America* (Philadelphia: Fortress Press, 1984) 30.

[3]See especially James W. Gustafson's essay in this volume.

[4]A. Whitten and Z. Sardar, "Master Plan for a Tropical Paradise," *New Scientist* 93 (23 July 1981): 230–35.

[5]See B. M. Boom, "Amazon Indians and the Forest Environment," *Nature* 6 (1985): 314, 324; and B. M. Boom, 'Advocacy Botany' for the Neotropics, in *Garden* 9:3 (1985b): 24–32.

[6]See W. E. Kerr and D. A. Posey, "Inormacoes Adicioais sobre a Agricultura dos Kayapo," *Intercinecia* 9 (1984): 392–400.

[7]1 Kings 4:33–34.

[8]Proverbs 30:24–28.

[9]Job 12:7–9.

# Chapter 3

# Ecofarming and Landownership in Ghana

## by Robert Clobus

On 3 March 1983, I was working with my people on a community project not far from the coast. The weather was very dry. The sky was hazy with the fine dust of a harmattan that had stayed longer than people had ever experienced before. Slowly but steadily, a dry and hot wind grew in strength, carrying with it fumes of smoke and the scent of burnt grass. It was the time for burning farm plots, and all around the area isolated columns of smoke could be seen. As the smoke thickened and the wind increased, people became restless and stopped working, staring around them and pointing at fires all over the countryside. Isolated fires joined, and all at once a great fire was nearby; it dawned on us that something never seen before and terrible was happening. The whole countryside was in flames. An increasingly strong and hot wind blew smoke and ashes past us. Work came to a halt. Many people were frightened, mumbling to themselves that the end of the world had come. Later on, I heard that on that day a large section of Ghana and part of the Ivory Coast burned, leaving a land of ashes.

On 13 March 1985, early risers in Navrongo—a town in the north of Ghana—woke up to another chilly dawn. The north was still in the grip of a severe harmattan. Suddenly, nature became ominously silent. Hens stopped chattering, and the sky darkened again. Softly but steadily a rustling wind, carrying fine dust with it, started blowing. The powdery sand penetrated everything and made it difficult for people to keep their eyes open. People sat with their backs toward the wind, covering their mouths and noses. They huddled around small fires that flickered with a strange bluish color, waiting for the first sandstorm they had ever witnessed to subside. In parts of the north, this storm lasted for more than eight hours.

Ghana is not a country where people are starving or thirsting more than in Ethiopia or the Sudan or Burkina Fasso, which is on Ghana's doorstep. But something is amiss; something is terribly wrong. Firestorms and sandstorms! Ghana is drying up. Nature is faltering. And why? Because of the doings of persons.

"Am I my brother's keeper?" Cain asked God. Must I keep the Earth for my fellow human beings? we may well ask ourselves. A traditional ruler in Ghana once said: "Land belongs to a vast family of whom many are dead, a few are living and a countless host are still unborn."[1] It is for the unborn that I must plead today.

Ghana is situated on the west coast of Africa between the Ivory Coast on the west and Togo on the east. In the north it is bordered by Burkina Fasso, formerly called Upper Volta. It stretches from the coast upward, from about latitude five degrees north to beyond latitude eleven degrees north. Ghana covers an area of approximately 239,460 square kilometers—one-third is forest, two-thirds savanna area—and has a population of almost twelve million.[2] About fifty-six percent of the population is below the age of fifteen, sixty-four percent under the age of twenty, and ninety percent under the age of forty-five. The annual growth in population is a little below three percent.

The greater part of the peasant population consists of subsistence farmers who, after a period of relative prosperity, are now going through a very difficult time in trying to survive on what rain-fed agriculture gives them. The infrastructure—consisting of good roads, transport, and a fair pricing system for food and farming products—has collapsed. Loans for the small farmer are difficult to secure. The government keeps the prices of foodstuffs low in order to appease the urban population. Most often, the small land-holder does not own the soil that is farmed, and he can thus be ejected from this land without compensation. More and more land near roads and water courses is being appropriated for state farms or has been leased by the authorities to companies for mechanized farming.

Land for the small farmer has become so scarce (especially in the Greater Accra, Eastern, and Central Region of Ghana) that people cannot afford to let the land rest. They use it over and over again, burning the scanty grass that grows on it when the dry season comes to an end. Land that used to be fertile is now only good for planting cassava. Cash crops like cocoa have offered so little reward of late that many farmers have lost interest in their growth.[3] They now cut down the shade trees that were a dominant feature on all cocoa farms and sell the wood as firewood. The effect of this tree felling has been very dramatic. Areas that were forested a few years ago now resemble wasteland, with only a few isolated orange or mango trees left. I have been walking the countryside for a good twenty years and previously could go from village to village under a canopy of trees. Now I can look two to three miles ahead and see the rusty tin roofs of the neighboring village surrounded by coconut palms.

In the north, the original savanna has been enlarged by the "derived" savanna,[4]—an environment wherein most trees have been eliminated. With the loss of these trees, the groundwater level has fallen more than eight meters within the past fifteen years, causing the death of more trees.[5] Through overgrazing and overcultivation, the grass cover is also disappearing. On top of all this—and maybe because of it—the rigors of the dry season come earlier, stay longer, and are more severely felt.[6]

The rainfall in the north has always been marginal for agriculture but has now become even more erratic. It makes any crop cultivation a risky enterprise for the poor farmer who has lost all his reserves through previous years of drought.[7] The price of failure in such circumstances is not bankruptcy but starvation. In the face of rising food shortages, the government and donor organizations are promoting large-scale mechanized farming. Funds are readily available for such enterprises, but they do not solve the food problem.[8] The peasant man and woman are left out of all these schemes. They are considered a relic of the past, a hindrance to Ghana's emergence among the advanced nations.

There is a growing awareness, especially in government circles, that humans have disturbed the balance: too many trees have gone; indiscriminate burning disrupts the environment and has an effect on the rainfall; an acute shortage of firewood is imminent.[9] There is, however, no clear policy determining how to solve these problems. The government is campaigning for trees to be planted, but the seedlings are often not there, or are available only in the midst of the dry season. People are encouraged to plant trees, but are not told which trees, when and where to plant them, or how to do it. Ghana is not a Sahelean country, but it is very much affected by the prevailing drought, and it has itself aggravated the situation squandering its natural resources.

What are the main factors that have contributed to the present situation? The natural growth of the population, especially along the coast, coupled with the coastal savanna-type climatic conditions that have made farming only marginally possible, has laid claim to all arable land to feed the growing population. To cite one example, the population of the capital Accra rose from 20,000 in 1911 to 60,000 in 1931, to more than one million at present in the Accra-Tema conglomerate. Not only did those people have to be fed, they needed firewood and building materials and made a heavy demand on natural resources. This situation led to an almost complete deforestation and denudation of the southeastern coastal area.[10]

The traditional farming technique used, namely rotational bush fallow,[11] added to the problem by laying claim to a larger section of the land than was actually under cultivation. Mechanized farming added to the problem by clearing large stretches and ploughing them over and over again. In this way, the texture of the soil was changed, which caused a decrease in its potential fertility and in its water-holding capacity.

Unfortunately, resource mismanagement has been going on unchecked since the arrival of early humans in Ghana. During the last pluvial—which succeeded a period of severe drought around 11,000 years ago—Ghana was clothed with a dense forest that was open in the north and on the southeastern coastal plains. In the interpluvial—the drier period which followed—the forest was thinned out on its northern and southeastern edges, leaving an open forest. It was around this time, about 8,000 years ago, that Neolithic persons came to stay.[12] Sufficient historical evidence exists to substantiate the former presence of more luxuriant vegetation in the coastal savanna belt. The same can be said for the north, where forested fetish groves break the monotony of the present-day grass cover. Human cultivation habits have made a deep impact on the environment in those ecologically sensitive areas of the savanna from the moment that cattle rearing, land cultivation, and burning vegetation to facilitate hunting were introduced.[13]

The forest area became really settled from the thirteenth century onward. From then on, humans made a lasting imprint on their physical environment.[14] This impact became obvious in northern Ghana and on the southeastern coastal plains where the wood cover was almost completely eliminated. Today, only the names of towns and villages on the coastal plains remind us of their original close association with the forest.[15]

The process of deforestation has had its ups and downs, synchronized with war and peace and with periods of epidemics and relative health.[16] Deforestation became more systematic after the first half of the nineteenth century when the commercial timber industry and cocoa farming became established. From 1910 onward, the attack on the forest became even more severe through the combined demands of the growing timber and mining industries, road and railway construction, the increase in population, and the spread of cash crop farming.[17] But food farming was and still is the greatest single cause of deforestation.[18]

Around the turn of the century, with the introduction of machinery, mechanized farming became possible. This type of farming also made a heavy demand on the environment. Large areas of land were stripped of all vegetation and replanted with either perennial crops such as the oil palm or were used seasonally for cash crops like maize, cassava, and rice. All those crops were grown in monocultures to facilitate pest and disease control and harvesting; those persons in charge were most often unfamiliar with the fragile nature of tropical soils. Land that looked fertile because of the lush vegetation it sustained was hastily bared and leveled, ploughed and planted, but ceased to produce well after two or three farming seasons because of the intimate relationship in tropical areas between the soil and the living matter it sustains. Destroy the living matter and you have broken the cycle of give and take existing in the ecosystem.

Tropical rainstorms, followed by scorching sunshine, degrade the soil, and in no time land that could sustain a forest deteriorates into an eroded, leached, and caked land that is not even able to sustain weeds.[19] There are, in other words, inherent dangers in attempting large-scale farming on sensitive tropical forest and savanna soils, but the awareness of these dangers has not yet penetrated those government and donor circles where far-reaching policy decisions on behalf of the Third World are being made.

In addition to a natural shortage of land and resource mismanagement as contributing factors to the present crisis is the persistent drought situation in many parts of Africa, particularly in the Sahel and its bordering region. A 1983 publication released in the United States entitled "Environmental Change in the West African Sahel" clearly shows drought to be a regular phenomenon in that region. The Sahel is a zone 200-400 kilometers wide, centered on latitude fifteen degrees north.[20] Drought has struck here repeatedly during past ages and has happened at least six times since 1400. The chances for it to occur come about three times a century. It occurred around 1910 and has been a climatic factor since 1968. Past records show that such droughts tend to last from ten to fifteen years. As yet, there is no way of predicting these periods.

From past records, it is obvious that the rainfall in the Sahel is generally low and that drought is an inherent feature. When a wet period occurs, pasturalists and farmers tend to follow the rain northward and to occupy land that, because of its marginal suitability, should have been left untouched. This occupation of critical areas took place in many Sahelean countries in the 1950s. At that time, the number of cattle increased fivefold in the western Sahel. After the rains had subsided, immediate overgrazing and overcultivation began in an area that was already critical for sustaining life.[21]

Drought cannot be escaped. It is a natural feature for the Sahel and has a direct influence on the rainfall in the regions bordering it. Experts disagree considerably when they discuss the causes of those recurring droughts. It has been observed, however, that whenever such droughts do occur, other parts of Africa are affected by similar weather patterns.[22] Thus, the interesting question is whether human beings have influenced the severity and the longevity of drought as it occurs now. Some recent studies indicate that the answer may be yes.

Can it be said, therefore, that the impact of the present drought increased as a consequence of changes in land use brought about by that same drought? J. G. Charney first proposed this hypothesis in 1975, suggesting that Sahelean rainfall is strongly influenced by biogeophysical feedback—meaning that drought can easily reinforce itself through the changes it evokes in the Sahelean land surface due to natural or human-made devegetation.[23] Reduced ground cover can result in a reduction of rainfall. It has been suggested that one-third to two-thirds of all rainfall in the Sahel is derived from re-evaporated soil moisture within the region. It is therefore possible—if not probable—that the present drought is overstaying its natural period because of changes brought about by the human impact on the environment.

Ecofarming may be the answer to the question of how to restore the relation between the Earth and humanity, but what are the possibilities of its implementation in Ghana?[24] Ecofarming is an Earth-friendly way of growing plants for human needs in which the demands made on the Earth are compensated for by the goods returned to it. Where the relation between humanity and Earth has been disturbed, ecofarming intends to restore the balance.

Is ecofarming an altogether new concept for the Ghanaian farmer? The evidence indicates that traditional Ghanaian society has always possessed an ecological awareness.[25] People considered the Earth a feeding mother who had to be remembered every day and invoked when people prayed. Indeed, Ghanaians believed it was necessary to ask the Earth's permission to touch her whenever farming began. The newly born were laid on the bare earth and the dead were entrusted to her. In south Ghana the Earth was called Asaase Efua or Asaase Yaa, meaning a most powerful goddess—not equal to the sky god, but more important in many ways because nobody could do without her in daily life. She was the caretaker who distributed and received back; she was helpful when appeased, harmful if neglected. All over Ghana, land use was a borrowing act for which one rendered continuous thanks.

According to traditional ideas, land belongs to the family. This concept made the living the temporary possessors of a heritage that was destined to pass to generations yet unborn. Land was also the sanctuary of departed ancestors and belonged to them as much as to future generations. Land was an ancestral trust; it was the most valuable heritage of the community and could not be sacrificed. People were well aware of their status as users only. An Ashanti saying goes: "The farm is mine but the soil belongs to the stool."

The "stool" is a seat carved out of a single piece of wood. In the case of a chief, it symbolizes the power of his office. A chief's stool was believed to incorporate the soul of the nation by being very close to the ancestral spirits and the land they own. When a chief died, if his reign was good, his stool would be preserved and added to the number of stools from previous chiefs that were kept in a special room. The stool was intended to represent what the dead and the living own together.

How much of this balanced view is still alive today? The sudden contact with foreigners, Western ideas, technology, and—not the least—Christianity severely disrupted the old order without creating a clear alternative. The disruption is noticeable in people's attitude toward land nowadays. In the old order, land was plentiful and was kind to its tillers: that is, wherever people went, land would be available. Farming was simple. It was a question of cutting down the bush, waiting a few days, burning the leaves, planting, doing some weeding, and then harvesting the food. Nobody sought to maintain the fertility of the soil other than by letting the land rest after two or three years of cultivation. Now the land has no time to rest and must produce every time. Many farmers are disheartened because the soil has stopped producing. But only a few farmers attribute the cause of this problem to overuse of the soil.

Whenever I talk about this situation with friends in the villages, I ask them: "Is it fair to take away from the land, day after day, without ever returning thanks to the soil for what it has given you?" The only Ghanaian practice that resembles ecofarming is intercropping, but it is done only in regard to vegetable plots. Maize, cassava, and rice are grown by everybody in the white man's way—in monocultures. As a result of what has been tried so far, the land has become infertile. People are at a loss. They have no choice but to use the same piece of land over and over again; what else can they do?

I have been trying to demonstrate to farmers that if they cultivate one-quarter of the land they have and use the leaves and debris of the other three-quarters for green manuring and mulching, they will spend less energy and harvest more than if they had cultivated the whole plot. They look at me, smile, and say: "You white men have your own way of doing things and we have ours." Somehow the link with Aberewa, "the Old Lady," has been severed.

For several years now—since my own conversion—I have tried to create a new ecological awareness by teaching friends how to revitalize the soil. The most promising group I meet regularly consists of about fifty catechists. They are local preachers from Catholic communities in the villages—mostly young men—who come together once monthly for some basic training in all kinds of social and catechetical skills. Ecofarming is now a regular feature on the program. It was at one of those meetings, after a fervent plea to plant Leuceuna trees on their plots of land, that one young man stood up and remarked: "But, Father, what is the use of improving the land you work on, if the land is not yours?" A general murmur of approval followed. It became clear that almost none of those present worked on land that they could call their own. Unfortunately, this question about who owns the land may prove a major obstacle for the implementation of ecofarming.

It is not uncommon in this day to see people ejected from land that they and their relatives have been working on for decades, shifting from plot to plot. They are told: "The chief needs the land for something," or "a big man from Accra has come for the land," or "the government needs the land to grow pineapples to earn foreign exchange." There is no other way for average persons but to quit. They have never been made aware of their rights as human beings, as children of the land. They do not know the law, and even if they know it, they do not have the means to pay for its enforcement. Land ownership is secure for the financially strong, but very much insecure for those who depend on the chief or the family for land on which to work.

A related problem is the inheritance system among the "Akan"—a cluster name for a group of people who are related culturally and linguistically and make up forty percent of the total population in the south.[26] The Akan trace their blood ties only through their mother. As in all traditional societies, the male wields the power in a family, but since family membership comes from the mother, he inherits from his mother's brothers and not from his natural father.

If a man dies intestate, his property reverts to his mother's family. Some consideration will be shown to the wife and children of the deceased, but they have no right to any of his possessions. Many times have I seen a wife being ejected from the house she stayed in with her husband until his death. This system of family property and inheritance has been under constant attack since the first missionaries arrived at the then-Gold Coast colony in the mid-eighteenth century. The first missionaries saw the acquisition of personal wealth through trading and cash crop farming as an effective way to undermine the hold that the extended family has over individuals. Today many educated people challenge the right of the extended family to exert its influence over the nuclear family in matters of personally acquired wealth and of inheritance. The system also has its merits, however. In it, people who otherwise would have been isolated and scattered in a rapidly changing world are held together through bonds of loyalty and interdependence.

What has been the attitude of the government? The British colonial government had always been in favor of minimal involvement in land ownership. At the same time, the European concept of acquisition of personal wealth through trading and cash crop farming became an established reality.[27] The postindependence governments have, from the onset, felt differently about individual ownership, especially with regard to land. They claim that too much abuse of power can be attributed to private ownership. Legislation since independence has been in the direction of making the state the owner of all unencumbered stool land and all natural resources. It would be an oversimplification to state that the present system of ownership and inheritance will lead to self-destruction. It is also wrong to credit the extended family system with sufficient strength to solve the present dilemma.

A subsistence economy has now been replaced by a money economy.[28] Ghana's population has doubled within the last fifty years. Old bastions of traditional authority are disintegrating: the chief, elders, the stool, and the traditional council of elders have little significance in the new political order. Gradually, land has been coming under the control of the government. Strong communal feelings that bind the family together persist while new forms of solidarity develop. Can ecofarming on a nationwide scale (otherwise it is meaningless) be implemented? What is the place of families therein? Can communal loyalty be strengthened while ensuring the rights of parents to work for their children and their children's children? Is commercial agriculture the best answer to feeding the growing population of Ghana? Traditional authority has degenerated, but has political authority gained any significance? These are all questions that cry for an immediate answer because of the lateness of the hour.

The last vestiges of traditional authority are centered around land ownership. When these vestiges are gone, what will be left, and what will take their place? The need for ecofarming and the attempts to implement it expose one of the many dilemmas facing Ghanaian society. Once more, the old way of doing things will have to be abandoned without knowing for sure whether the new order will work and will keep society together. The temptation must be great for the government to confiscate all land and become the sole and permanent owner of the soil.

At the present moment, Ghana is very close to the South American situation in which people are landless yet labor on their own land.[29] More and more land ends up in the hands of a few people.[30] There is a great temptation to argue that the need for increased food production and the instances of land misuse justify wholesale land appropriation. But this would mean the end of the Ghanaians' independence! The strength of a nation lies in its freedom—and not just territorial freedom but the liberty to follow its own direction. What is our choice? What do we value most as a nation, as Christians? Is it more important to have material prosperity comparable to that of the Western world or to have a proud and independent way of life based on traditional values in communion with each other and with the Earth? Where are the Christians at this critical hour?

Ignoring for practical reasons the attempts of Catholic Portuguese missionaries four centuries earlier, the missionary effort in Ghana starts in earnest with the arrival of the Basel Mission around 1820. From the beginning, the missionaries were bent on isolating converts from their families and cultural surroundings by housing them in Salems, a type of ghetto, and by giving them a new set of values.[31] As a means of making individuals economically independent of their families, they promoted trade, crafts, and cash crop farming. The early stress on private initiative greatly contributed to the spread of cash crops such as cotton, coffee, and cocoa.[32]

The early Basel missionaries worked among the Akwapim, an ethnic group in the eastern region of Ghana. It was those farmers who, realizing the potentialities of cocoa growing, migrated inland in search of land. They succeeded in buying land from chiefs in the forest areas, notwithstanding traditional concepts about land ownership. Now, many of these poorly documented land transactions are being challenged in the courts.[33]

Cocoa cultivation became a great success; the total export of cocoa rose from thirteen tons in 1895 to more than 50,000 tons in 1914, to 220,000 in 1926. The need for properly trained administrators very soon gave rise to the establishment of schools. The stress on formal education outweighed the importance attached to crafts and farming. By the late 1960s, it became apparent that the supply of clerks was more than the country could absorb. During the last decade, more importance has again been laid on the teaching of crafts and the promotion of farming and livestock rearing. But Ghana now has a several generations of dropouts who despise farming and dislike all manual work. Only during the last few years has a new appreciation grown for the farmer and for the contribution he makes to the nation. Not too long ago, ecology was an unknown word, as was the case in the West. Today, more institutes are open to teach crafts and help small-scale farmers make a living on their land. The small-scale approach necessitates new ways of farming—ways that are less mechanized and more adapted to local practices. The churches are playing an active role in this new effort.

At this very moment, the new global ecological awareness is slowly finding expression in isolated efforts by churches and church-sponsored individuals to do something about the environment in Ghana. In 1982, the Catholic Church published a pamphlet entitled "Desertification in Ghana," pointing to the dangers of deforestation and indiscriminate burning. At this moment, several church-sponsored water borehole projects are being implemented. But, more important, tree-planting projects sponsored by churches have also been going on for the past few years. The Salvation Army in Ghana has a well-organized Farmers' Training Program centered around the idea of agroforestry, with special emphasis on the introduction of the leucaena tree. They train field officers and provide supervision and inoculants for the seeds. This Christian group has an excellent program, with a good training scheme, but lacks a countrywide infrastructure to execute the program.

Just imagine the effect were the Catholic Church—or better still, all churches—to have such a program! If the churches were to embark on the introduction of agroforestry, it would take them about a year to form a cadre of instructors who would then train field officers. Within two years, demonstration plots could be planted in all the rural communities of Ghana. To my knowledge, outside of the Salvation Army, no such effort by either the Catholic Church or any other churches is being contemplated.

Right now we must define for whom we want to work, what we want to achieve, and how we want to do it. Did Christ not say, "I have come to seek out those who are lost" (Luke 19:10)? We must identify ourselves with the plight of small farmers, uphold their right to an independent living, and help them to achieve it. But the churches are easily inclined to identify with and opt for the middle and upper classes. A lot of soul searching will have to be done.

What do we want to achieve? The unprotected subsistence farmers, after paying for Ghana's precolonial and postcolonial development, are now in danger of being sacrificed for the sake of ill-conceived economic development. Ministers talk about a new heaven and a new Earth and about life after death, while life on Earth is made increasingly impossible for the farmers. Must we Christians ignore our present home? We must keep the Earth, treasure it, and give it new life.

But how is this to be done? Churches could start by uniting as one. They could concentrate on the urban areas,

where so many youngsters go and lose hope. Our prime
Christian task may lie in the towns, but we should also
anticipate the hour when the towns decline by revitalizing
the rural areas with health, better housing, job opportunities,
and amenities for job satisfaction. Most important of all, the
environment in which we live must be revived and stabilized
so that the rains may continue to fall and the soil continue to
provide food for those who work on it. The churches can
involve themselves. They have excellent infrastructures at
their disposal enabling them to bring expertise and know-
how to the smallest rural community.

What can I do as an individual when so much that goes
wrong  seems completely beyond the control of one person
or even all humanity? What can I do where there is so much
work to be done and so little time to do it? Am I my brother's and sister's keeper? Must I feel responsible for the
wrongdoings of others?

I have always loved nature and have walked in it with an
open eye. I was indifferent, however, to the blindness of
others while enjoying myself. Now I have become aware that
the nature I enjoy is disappearing and will not come back if
I and others do not find a way to preserve it. I was at a loss
as to what to do and where to begin. Then I met a man who,
in his own small way, makes little gardens in a desert world
and is content with doing just that. He explained the power
of the sign to me. When night is dark and nothing can be
seen, a spark of light restores hope that a new day will break.
When nobody sees a way out and accepts a given situation
as unchangeable, it is that one spark, that one question, that
one remark, that one refusal to accept defeat that leads one
on. When everybody says that it cannot be done, and one
does it, all those who seek have found.

A sign is a bit like the Cross. It is of necessity isolated,
out of place—a sign of hope and ridicule at the same time. It
is misunderstood or dismissed by many as irrelevant. But
some people will recognize it as a beacon they have been

looking for all their lives. What I want to do is to bring about signs of hope: small gardens that will shine up as green lights of hope in a land of yellow dryness. These signs would prove to people that there is a way of living with God's Earth. It is possible and good to keep the Earth, treasure it, and make it flower and produce a hundredfold.

Christ spoke to his apostles in words that have a very special meaning for me and which, I pray, will have meaning for all missionary earthkeepers. "You did not choose me, no, I chose you; And I commissioned you to go out and bear fruit, fruit that will last" (John 15:16). Are those words not meant as an encouragement and as a challenge to all churches to gather themselves together and to go out of their temples of worship and bear fruit? It is the bearing of fruit that matters, fruits that will last.

# Bibliography

Asante, S. K. B. *Property Law and Social Goals in Ghana, 1844–1966.* Accra: Ghana University Press, 1975.

Boahen, Adu. *Topics in West African History.* London: Longmans, 1964.

Cloudsley-Thompson, J. L. *Man and the Biology of Arid Zones.* Baltimore: University Park Press, 1977.

de Vos, Antoon. *Africa, the Devastated Continent: Man's Impact on the Ecology of Africa.* The Hague: W. Junk, 1975.

*Desertification in Ghana.* Ghana: Justice and Peace Commission of the Catholic Church, 1982.

Dickson, Kwamina B. *A Historical Geography of Ghana.* London: Cambridge University Press, 1969.

Egger, Kurt. *Methoden und Möglichkeiten des "Ecofarming" in Berglandern Ostafrikas.* Heidelberg, Germany: Botanisches Institut der Universität Heidelberg.

Engman, E. V. *Outlines of the Population of Ghana, 1960–1970.* University Coast, 1975.

*Environmental Change in the West African Sahel.* Advisory Committee on the Sahel, Board on Science and Technology for International Development, Office of International Affairs, National Research Council, U.S.A. Washington D.C.: National Academy Press, 1984.

Gei Danyuah, Kwabena. *The History of Land Legislation.* Daily Graphic Survey, 1985.

Ghana, *Landen documentatie*, No. 5. Amsterdam: Royal Institute for the Tropics, 1982.

Hayden, Thomas, S. M. A., and Richard Massaro. *Hunger and Starvation in Africa*. Washington D.C.: S. M. A. Social Concerns Department, 1985.

Hill, Polly. *Migrant Cocoa Farmers of Southern Ghana*. London: Cambridge University Press, 1963.

Morgan, W. B., and J. C. Pugh. *West Africa*. London: Methuen & Co., 1969.

*National Geographic* 63:1 (1983), 2–64.

Nicholson, Sharon. *The Climatology of Sub-Saharan Africa*. Washington D.C.: National Academy Press, 1983.

Odamtten, S. K. *The Missionary Factor in Ghana's Development (1820–1880)*. Accra: Waterville Publishing House, 1978.

Ofiri, I. M., ed. *Factors of Agricultural Growth in West Africa*. Legon, 1973.

Pugh, J. C., and A. E. Perry. *A Short Geography of West Africa*. London: University of London Press, 1960.

Reynolds, Edwards. *Trade and Economic Change on the Gold Coast, 1807–1874*. London: Longmans, 1974.

Weischet, Wolfgang. *Schwierigkeiten tropischer Bodenkultur*. Spektrum der Wissenschaft, (1984) 112–122.

Wood, G. A. R. *Cocoa*. London: Longmans, 1975.

Young, Luise B. *Earth's Aura*. Middlesex: Penguin Books,1977.

# Notes

[1]Nana Ser Ofori Alta I, Omanhene of Akim Abuakwea.

[2]Of this forest area, 20,000 km² consists of forest reserve and unprotected forest; 62,590 km² is being used for food and cash crops. Of the savanna,90,000 km² is reserve and unprotected areas, while 62,590 km² is being used for food and cash crops. In 1950, 51% of the forest was left; at present, 18% of the forest is left.

[3]From 1911 to 1977, Ghana was the biggest producer of cocoa. In 1981, the Ivory Coast was first with 420,000, Brazil was second with 305,000, and Ghana was third with 280,000. In 1960, the producer got 65% of the export price; in 1966/67, 53%; in 1972/73, 44%; and in 1977/78, 37%. The price the producer gets has generally increased, but it is not known what percent of the export price this represents.

[4]The extension of grassland by setting fire to vegetation may have give risen to the derived savanna, which may be found locally as far as six degrees north. These derived savannas are matched by the "fringing forests" and "galary forests" found in the Guinea Savanna.

[5]This level was lower than during the medieval period.

[6]Rainfall almost everywhere in West Africa shows much greater unreliability than in the British Isles, for example. The greatest variation from mean values is in the months at the beginning and end of the wet season.

[7]It seems that for pastoral people, the limiting isopleth is that of seven months of complete drought; for agricultural people the normal limit is five and one-half to six months of drought.

[8]In 1980 the F. A. O. declared Ghana a "food-deficit" country.

[9]The significance of the issue led *The Graphic* to devote two pages of a recent issue of its Saturday edition to the environment and peasant farming.

[10]At the margins of the Closed Forest, including the Accra plains, the original vegetation was probably an open forest featuring the *antiaris chlorophora* of the Closed Forest. It was probably succeeded further north by a deciduous forest. In North Ghana scattered fetish groves, up to five acres in extent, break the monotony of the grassland cover. Experiments in northern Ghana have shown that complete protection of the Guinea Savanna vegetation ensures rapid development toward a closed woodland and a forest type of climate. Furthermore, there is historical evidence, applying to the coastal areas only, to indicate the former presence of more luxuriant vegetation. See *A Historical Geography of Ghana*, 337–38.

[11] It depends on the development of fallows, which are never allowed to revert to woodland. The area of fallows must normally be greater than the area planted and consist of self-sown plants, grasses, or shrubs, on land formerly devoted to crops. Grassy fallows, woody fallows: both cultivators employ crop mixtures, rotation, and successions.

[12]*A Historical Geography of Ghana*, 35. The rudimentary form of cultivation practiced existed side by side with hunting and food collecting and was for centuries subordinate to them. Neolithic culture had far-reaching consequences in the natural landscape.

[13]The southward movement of the vegetation zone due to human influence has probably been continuous for thousands of years. Northward, the vegetation thins out to nothing. Southward, the savanna gives place to high forest except in the coastal zone from eastern Ghana to southern Benin, where the vegetation reaches the sea.

Ancient and medieval societies had a substantial impact through activities such as setting brushfires, producing charcoal for local needs, iron smelting, and the establishment of settlements on early destabilized sites (cf. *Environmental Change in the West African*

*Sahel*, 2).

The results of brush fires are a reduction and simplification of vegetation, soil depletion through losses of nitrogen, reduced nutrient cycling through deep-rooted trees and shrubs, and critical breakdowns in soil ecology (Ibid., 25).

In areas where cattle are maintained, these fires in turn characteristically result in the overgrazing of the perennial grasses, a further reduction of biological productivity, and declining carrying capacity. Cattle are generally replaced by goats and sheep and, finally, when the grasslands have been reduced to desert, camels gain in importance. The transition from woodland to desert has occurred within living memory in many parts of Africa. (cf. Cloudsley Thompson, *Man and the Biology of Arid Zones*).

[14]As in the northern zones of West Africa, human influence on the forest in recent centuries has changed totally the nature and character of vegetation and of the soil. The continued existence of original high forest anywhere in West Africa is doubtful. Probably the whole of the present forest area has been cultivated at one time or another, with secondary growth over farm clearings. 214.

[15]*A Historical Geography of Ghana*, 338. Potsin, the name of a large village situated in the grassy plains behind Winneba, means "a stretch of forest." In central Togo, close to the Ghana border, are the Kabre, among whom are found the Hama. Hama is an abbreviation of *han-mba*, which means "people of the forest."

[16]Ibid., 58. Equally devastating were the numerous epidemics that periodically swept over the country. The two most deadly were smallpox and guinea worm disease, which Bosinan referred to as "national diseases." Within the last three decades of the seventeenth century, thousands of people perished through an epidemic of smallpox.

[17]In 1927, a forest ordinance was passed to preserve the forests of this country. In 1939, forest reserves amounted to 5,700 square miles, or nineteen percent of closed forest area.

[18]*A Historical Geography of Ghana*, 343. With 11,600 square miles

of forest computed to have been destroyed since 1894, it was concluded in 1934 that bush fallowing accounted for 10,600 square miles. The figures lay no claim to absolute accuracy, but they confirm that food farming was the most widespread occupation and, in view of the techniques of cultivation, then fire was the main agent of deforestation.

[19]Here I mean indigenous weeds. A new weed has completely taken over the countryside in southern Ghana. It is the *Eupatorium Microstemma*, a composite first gathered in 1953. It emerged as a dominant weed on all farms around 1972 and was given the local name of the then-living general Acheampiny. All fallow land nowadays is covered by this weed. Whether this weed is advantageous as a cover crop has not yet been fully studied.

[20]Today the term *Sahel* has been more broadly applied to non-Sahelean regions of the member states of the Permanent Interstate Committee for drought control in the Sahel (C.I.L.S.S.). The states include Cape Verde, Senegal, The Gambia, Mauritania, Mali, Upper Volta, Niger, and Chad. In these states the Sahel proper covers approximately two million square kilometers (*History of the Geography of Ghana* 9).

Some dune records indicate that desert conditions extended an average three degrees latitude farther south than is the case today. But such extreme aridity has not been experienced during the last 12,500 years. Latitudinal shifts since about 1950 have been comparatively limited in extent. Tentative conclusions are that the Sahel probably experienced wetter conditions in the ninth through thirteenth centuries and that these wetter conditions declined sometime during the fourteenth century.

[21]The wet conditions of the 1950s promoted use of more marginal lands. Conditions changed abruptly around 1960, and rainfall continually declined until 1973. It is commonly thought that the drought ended in the mid-1970s, but a recent analysis of more current data contradicts this opinion. Relatively dry conditions have persisted for approximately two decades, and it now appears that this century may be the driest one in the Sahel and its borderlands in more than 1,000 years. Ibid., 21.

Cattle are poorly adapted to Sahelean conditions; their conversion efficiency is poor; they require substantial quantities of water; and they are highly subject to stress. Cattle increase pressure on perennial grasses and often eliminate them (because they are grazers and not browsers). Ibid., 34

[22]Ibid., 88. Abnormal conditions in the Sahel tend to be coupled with abnormal conditions in the analogous semiarid regions of Southern Africa.

[23]*Environmental Change in the West African Sahel*, 43. Ecosystems in tropical arid and semiarid regions "renew" themselves only as long as sufficient species diversity is maintained to prevent the collapse of the system. Below a certain threshold, there is a dramatic domino effect with regard to species loss within an ecosystem.

[24]Ibid., 44. The restoration of biological diversity and ecosystem function in basic environmental rehabilitation effects sustainable production in the Sahel. Declining biological diversity and productivity also threaten the adaptive and evolutionary capabilities of plant and animal species, reduce the viability of Sahelean agra-silvo-pastoral systems, and characteristically lead to economic, social, and political instability.

[25]*Property Law and Social Goals in Ghana, 1844–1966*, 2-6.

[26]Akan–44%; Mole-Dagbane–16%; Ewe–13%; Ga-Adangbe–8.5%.

[27]Kwabena Gei Danyuah, *The History of Land Legislation* (Daily Graphic Survey, 1985). The opposition to land legislation itself can be seen as an attempt by a cash conscious minority of the educated elite who had been envious of the new status and wealth of the chiefs, which they attributed to the British as a means of opposing British rule. With the change in the relationship between chiefs and the people as a result of industrialism, the resources of "stool lands" (which were meant for the whole community) came to be the preserve of the chiefs. The idea that each family had or was entitled to a piece of land has also become impossible to uphold.

[28]*Property Law and Social Goals in Ghana, 1844-1966*, 185, 186. Traditionalism survives in various forms. The strong communal feeling that bound the families together persists, notwithstanding modern encroachments. The trusteeship idea serves as a useful ethical standard, eroded but not erased. New forms of group solidarity have been devised, and the traditional spirit of cooperation survives, seeking new outlets. The notion of ancestral ownership of basic property, especially land, underlined the community interest in all property. The labor theory of property was incompatible with derivation of property from ancestors. What, then, should be the standing of individualism in modern Ghana? Does this scheme of values that adequately served traditional Ghana have any meaning for modern Ghana?

[29]Ibid., 240. Within the past decades, many Latin American countries have been thrown into violent social convulsions by the gross disparity in land ownership. On the one hand are the fragmentary parcels, held by peasants who are barely able to subsist on their holdings, while on the other hand are the unwieldy estates, mainly concentrated in the hands of absentee owners, who let their property to peasant farmers at exorbitant prices. This explosive situation ignites into conflagration when the underprivileged, in exasperation, take matters into their own hands.

[30]Ibid., 241. S. K. Asante can still write, "Happily Ghana is free of this gross inequality of land ownership. Nevertheless the doctrinal foundations of such disparity are clearly discernible."

[31]*The Missionary Factor in Ghana's Development (1820–1880)*, 147. In 1880, the main industrial activities were developing in the country--one indigenous and the other new. Traditional industries were pottery, textiles, gold and other metal working, and boat building. New industries consisted of carpentry, joinery, cashmaking, and lockmaking. The Basel mission was responsible for the latter. These economic developments had social effects; they gave rise to a new middle class. In the new circumstances, the artisan and the merchant were becoming economically independent of the family. What seemed to happen was that parents and heads of families and of states began to surrender some authority

to the economically independent educated persons who therefore began to play an important social and political role. Before a 1865 Parliamentary Council, Shrenh said, "It is our resolution to make the Negroes independent." Steiner explains this point more clearly when he says that the aim in teaching industrial skills to Christian converts was to make them increasingly independent of the missions, of their own families, and—where appropriate—of their masters. Freeman's motives in launching his agricultural schemes were exactly the same (150). To help the converts throw away their traditional beliefs and practices, the missionaries at times adopted the policy of separating them socially as well as physically from the rest of the community. Christian quarters outside the town constituted a Salem—a shortened form of Jerusalem.

[32]S. K. B. Asante: Commercial agriculture therefore inaugurated permanent cultivation and disrupted the classical, *Ghana*, 21.

Important in those days was the growing influence of missionaries, especially the Basel Mission. The missionaries had a clear vision of what African society should look like after the abolition of slavery: a society sustained by small but prosperous farmers who, with the help of family or paid labor, grew export crops in exchange for European goods. They taught the population other new skills such as reading, writing, carpentry, and blacksmithing. They introduced new crops such as cocoa and coffee.

[33]"The farmer who has no security in Africa today is not the holder of the land as a member of a group but he who has acquired his land by cash transaction and does not know whether his claim is to be regarded as valid." I. M. Ofiri, ed., *Factors of Agricultural Growth in West Africa* (Legon, 1973).

Also recent land transactions and "sales" for large-scale farming are being legally challenged nowadays. George Bennels, "Land Tenure and Land Use," in *Factors of Agricultural Growth in West Africa*, lll: "After the 1966 coup the NLC government decided to hand over some of the state farms (which had been appropriated by the state without compensation) to private enterprise. One of these was the Minimaso State farm, which was acquired by the Pioneer Farms (Ghana), an American company. According to a report that appeared in the Pioneer, consideration fee of $10,000 was paid to the Ejuralene and his elders by the company for a leasehold of five miles square land. Some of the farmers who enjoyed the right to use part of the land for cultivation under the customary land-tenure system appear not to have been paid compensation. Hence, the transaction is being challenged. According to custom, the Ejuralene and his elders ought to have summoned the people by gong to get their consensus, but this was not done.

# Chapter 4

# The Environmental Impacts of a Church Project: A Zairian Village Case Study

## by Mutombo Mpanya

Interest in environmental problems encountered in the overseas work of Christian missions has accelerated with the recent African food crisis and with the threat of future crises. Many people assume that the food shortage was caused by poor traditional techniques of land management and the unwillingness or inability of the African nations to control birth rates. Others attribute the ecological crisis to the presence of large corporations looking for short-term profit. Some people falsely believe that since church agencies do not exploit natural resources such as oil and minerals, manufacture industrial products, or discharge their by-products into rivers, they do not create environmental problems.

Many traditional techniques of land exploitation used by Africans do have the potential to destroy the soil. For example, bush fire kills wild life indiscriminately while exposing the soil to rain, sun, and wind erosion. Overgrazing destroys the grass cover and leaves the soil unprotected. But many African people have also developed regenerative techniques for working on the land such as long fallow. In many places in Africa, the population has increased steadily during the past twenty years, but it is not clear that this increase is due to the traditional orientation toward fertility. Traditional wisdom about the spacing of children may well be undermined by Christian teachings that lead to larger families and higher population levels. The argument that large corporations exploiting natural resources are likely to create environmental problems is certainly true, but the focus of this chapter is the effect of church programs on the environment.

Church programs are thought to be small in size and by nature focused on education, health, and evangelization. While this description may be largely accurate, church programs also bring their own ways of exploiting the environment that have the potential to cause ecological problems in the local community. New methods of building and land cultivation, if not properly tested beforehand, can potentially destroy local soils. Desired outcomes of church programs may stimulate unintended adverse effects on the environment. The case study presented below exposes the environmentally detrimental effects of many church programs.

## The Case of Bakwa Mulumba

This case study involves the Bakwa Mulumba village and the Kalonda mission station in the Tshikapa area of central Zaire, near the Angolan border. Three sites were chosen to compare the density of trees and shrubs, the composition of catches from fishing, and the quality of the water. One of the sites included Bakwa Mulumba village and the mission station; the other two were about twenty to twenty-five miles north and south of the village, respectively. (The northern site was close to Bakwa Nsumpi, a Luba village of much the same size and demographic composition as Bakwa Mulumba.) These sites were similar in several ways. They all had the same soil and vegetation—wooden savannah of central Zaire; they were dominated by elephant grass and trees with the local name of *nkwanga*. All the sites included a small river with a large number of palm trees along its banks. These rivers were all tributaries of the Kasai River and were similar in length and flow.

Fifteen plots were studied, five in each of the three sites. Each plot was considered comparable on the basis of location and ecological conditions. In each plot, five independent assistants estimated the densities of grass cover and trees. Fishing was done in all three small rivers, and the results of the catches were compared. Fifty interviews were conducted with the people in the village on the subject of social and ecological changes. Many of the results were discussed with them. Based on this information, several estimates were made. The percentage of area covered by the tree canopies was used in calculating the density of tree cover. Samples of water were taken and checked every hour for cloudiness and silt deposit. Estimates of land use and the consumption of trees were based on direct observations and on interviews with villagers, including those who worked for the mission station.

## The Village and Its Resources

The village of Bakwa Mulumba, on the Kasai River, is part of a larger village called Kalonda. Bakwa Mulumba is situated between three rivers: namely, the Kasai River, the largest of the three located to the west of Bakwa Mulumba; the Mbumba River to the south; and the Kantobela River, to the north of the village and the smallest of the three rivers. Bakwa Mulumba has an altitude of about 700 meters or 2100 feet, a rainfall of close to 1,000 millimeters per year, and an average temperature that varies between twenty-five and thirty degrees centigrade. The soil, while mostly Kalahari sand, contains lateritic areas in the vicinity of the village. As a result, the mud walls of the houses are very red.

Bakwa Mulumba village was founded around 1910 when many Luba people moved into the Tshikapa region. These Luba people were escaping from the wars of slavery initiated by Ngongo Lutete, Lumpungu, and local leaders supported by the East African Arab slave traders. The Compagnie du Kasai, a colonial charter company, took advantage of the situation by facilitating the establishment of Bakwa Mulumba Village in order to create a labor reservoir in the area.

Initially, Bakwa Mulumba villagers worked as farmers; they also provided labor for the Companie du Kasai, cutting rubber and, later on, mining diamonds. A small percentage of the villagers worked in other businesses associated with the mining operations (e. g., transportation, storekeeping, hospitals, and schools). By 1950, Bakwa Mulumba was still a village of farmers who were living in a subsistence economy that had a small exchange sector.

Land is the most important resource at the disposal of the village and remains the main source of livelihood for almost all of the villagers. The villagers use about thirty to thirty-five square kilometers between the Mbumba, Tahimbinda, and Kasai Rivers. Within these limits, farmers must find their source of food, building material, firewood, and water.

Most of the food for the villagers comes from agriculture, animal husbandry, hunting, and gathering. Villagers grow a variety of crops including manioc, corn, peanuts, beans, and vegetables such as *aubergine, muteta, mulembwa, muhala,* and *mudibu.* Fruit trees include mango, papaya, orange, and lemon. Villagers raise sheep, goats, chickens, and other small livestock such as rabbits and ducks. They also hunt small wild game rodents (*nsenji, mpuku*) and birds (*mkwadi* and *makangala*). Several wild fruits grow on the land, including *ngaji katenda, mbulu,* and *matundu,* as well as other edibles such as mushrooms.

Villagers use trees and grass for building materials. Regular trees—mostly *nkwanga*—and palm trees are used to construct walls and roofs. Grass is used as thatch for the roof. The most abundant of the grasses, elephant grass, is sometimes used for the walls of temporary shelters. Dried grass and timber are burned as an essential source of fuel/energy.

The Kantobela River is used as a source of water for drinking and washing. Food such as manioc is processed in the Mbumba, Kantobela, Kangonga, and the Kaplonga Rivers. Fish are found mostly in the Kantobela and Kasai rivers. Villagers use several techniques to catch fish: line fishing mostly for small fish such as *misangi* and *bikela*; catch fishing for *tukunda* and *tusha*; and *kutuwa* fishing, a technique in which the people dam a river for a short period of time to expose the fish.

## The Mission Station

During 1952 and 1953 a mission station was established in Tshikapa for the purpose of evangelization. The location chosen for the station was near the Bakwa Mulumba village, between the Kasai River on the west and the Kantobela and Kangonga rivers on the south and north respectively.

After securing a concession for the station, the missionary built a small house for his family. The frame of the house was made of wood, as were the walls and the roof. Several classrooms were also constructed out of local materials—trees and thatch. By 1954-1955 the station had a modern dispensary and a primary school for more than 600 students constructed of brick with a tin roof. A Bible institute and ten other houses were built for expatriate personnel and some of the local workers. Over fifty families came from the surrounding areas to live on the station—some as workers and some because they desired to be closer to the school, the dispensary, or the church community.

Construction of the station called for foreign techniques that used local resources far in excess of those normally required in the construction of traditional structures. Large trees were cut into small pieces (one by fifteen inches) to be used as shingles to cover the roof and walls. Bricks were made of local clay and baked with energy supplied by wood fires. Some of the shelters built of local materials could contain more than 200 persons and were extremely imposing by traditional standards. Construction of these shelters increased the pressure on the local environment.

## Ecological Changes

In 1980 I visited the village of Bakwa Mulumba after being away for two decades and was received by an old woman who had known me as a boy in the village. As we discussed the changes that had occurred during the years, she concentrated specifically on some of the ecological trends. She complained that the land failed to produce as much as before, that crops no longer grew as easily as she remembered, that the river now had too much clay, and that women had to walk a long distance from the village to gather firewood or grow food.

Since memory is often unreliable, I did not know initially whether or not to believe her. Perhaps she was simply being nostalgic, and things were actually not very different. I also thought that some of those changes, if they had occurred, might have been caused by local agricultural practices such as bush fires.

After several weeks of research and observations in the village, however, it became clear that considerable ecological change had taken place during the past two decades. The ground cover in most places had been reduced substantially. Grass cover had dropped from ninety-six percent of the surface in 1960 to seventy-five percent in 1980. Regular trees that occupied one percent of the land surface in 1960 were only six-tenths of one percent in 1980. Palm trees had dropped from one-half of a percent to three-tenths of a percent. Wild fruits were almost completely eliminated, declining from six-tenths to two-tenths of one percent. The fishing catch was noticeably reduced as well: small sardines, or *tusangi*, had dropped from sixty-five to thirty-five percent of catches; *bikela* had declined from five percent to eight-tenths of one percent; *tukunda* fell from eight-tenths to three-tenths of one percent, and *tusha*, almost nonexistent now, went from three-tenths to one-tenth of one percent.

These ecological changes had several implications for other activities in the village economy. The decline in the number of palm trees, for example, had very significant consequences because of their numerous uses. Palm nuts and palm nut kernels are used to make oil. The male flower of the palm tree, if cut young, gives palm wine; when cut old, it is dried and burned so salt can be extracted from the ashes for seasoning food. The nervure of palm leaves is used as twine in the construction of brooms, fishing nets, and baskets for carrying many things, including small livestock. Salt and oil from palm trees are also used for medicinal purposes. The by-products of processed nuts and the dried parts of the palm tree are burned for fire. Thus, a decline in palm trees has numerous implications for a range of activities in the village economy.

Other important activities are also severely hindered by such ecological changes, including housing, which involves every group in the village—young and old, male and female. Construction of traditional houses requires grass, trees, palm trees, water, and clay. The size of housing units has decreased since 1960, probably as a result of the shortage of trees and other resources.

The ecological changes enumerated in the preceding paragraphs—namely, reduction in the number of trees and the amount of grass cover, as well as the increase in clay deposits in rivers—threaten the already delicate balance of available food. The number of people involved in agriculture has been reduced to one-half of what it was in 1960. Furthermore, those remaining in agriculture tend to be old people with declining physical energy. Agricultural technology, moreover, has not improved and actual agricultural productivity per acre and per person is declining. Animal husbandry has declined by seventy-five percent. The number of people involved in hunting and fishing has also declined.

Virtually no one is involved in hunting wild game. Very few people are still fishing (less than twenty-five percent of the total population). Wine making has been almost completely eliminated.

This reduction in food production is even more alarming if one looks at other aspects of the system. Traditional agriculture has been oriented toward subsistence and therefore results in very little surplus for exchange. The reduction of the number of people involved in agriculture—coupled with declining land and labor productivity—has created a situation in which people are depend on imported food. Traditional diets have been low but adequate in protein. The dramatic reduction of animal husbandry, fishing, and game hunting may cause protein deficiency in children and pregnant women. The reduction of palm trees and the consequent elimination of wine making has also contributed to insufficient protein and mineral salts in the people's diet. Thus, in reducing food availability and some essential elements of nutrition, the ecological crisis threatens the health of the population and undermines its physical capacity.

A point alluded to earlier bears repeating: these changes fostered economic dependency of the village on outside sources for survival. Here the outside consists of the international market, as can be illustrated by the shift in economic activities. Before 1950 agriculture was the most important activity in the village—involving almost ninety-five percent of the population. Between 1950 and 1980 a change occurred whereby most of the people in the village—namely young people—became students in the schools on the station. During this same period, general trade and diamond mining occupied most of the people in the village (more than seventy-five percent). The village became more dependent on the diamond trade and other trades that linked them to the international market. This would not have been so lamentable if the people had been paid adequately for the diamonds they mined. But, in fact, the wages are very low and fixed by multinational monopolies. Local villagers do not have the legal right to sell their diamonds to other buyers. Because of the declining productivity of land and labor, people have been forced to mine diamonds to survive. Once the diamond mines are exhausted or the wages fail to sustain a livelihood, the chances of starvation will increase. The mining of diamonds also increases the clay deposits in the rivers, thereby reducing the number of fish in the water.

An increase in the number of educated people does not necessarily ameliorate this situation. Young people enrolled in school forget traditional agricultural, food-producing, and gathering skills and do not acquire any other skill needed to survive in their community. Exacerbating this problem is their acquired desire for consumer goods and quick cash returns. Additionally, because of lower productivity in the agricultural sector and lack of opportunities in other areas, many young people are without any economic activity to sustain their lives. Many become unemployed, and some turn to crime or become alcoholics. These problems will certainly destroy the social structure of the village if existing trends continue.

We may identify three possible contributors to the ecological degradation that has taken place in the Bakwa Mulumba village. First, the traditional forms and rates of resource utilization may be at the root of the changes that have occurred. Setting bush fires for hunting, overgrazing, and *kutuwa* may have destroyed the soil and caused the deterioration of the environment. With a few exceptions, however, the traditional techniques of exploiting nature embodied elements of conservation and (for the most part) could not have created the ecological changes described above. Overpopulation could not have played a role because large numbers of young people left the village. What took place in the Bakwa Mulumba village was a rapid deterioration of the environment that could have been caused only by a new element in the ecological system.

Second, the mining company may have been the source of the environmental destruction. It is true that the mining operations needed a lot of wood for baking bricks, as energy for some of its trucks, and for home cooking. Neither the Kantobela nor Kangonga watershed areas, however, were used by the company for these purposes. These two watersheds were used mostly for agricultural purposes in the traditional manner. The mining company alone could not have affected the watersheds associated with the Bakwa Mulumba village to the extent that they were changed. The company may have indirectly had a negative impact in that it forced the villagers—through the colonial administration—to produce food for the local personnel of the company. To make farmers more productive, some aspects of production were changed slightly. Some elements of intensification in the agricultural practices may have undermined the soil. Generally speaking, however, the agricultural techniques used were still traditional and had strong conservational elements.

Third, the missionary station may have undermined the ecological situation of Bakwa Mulumba village. It caused a dramatic increase in the utilization of the village resources and introduced an educational system oriented toward western materialism rather than an agricultural life-style.

## Traditional Methods of Exploitation

With some limitations, the traditional methods of using natural resources in Bakwa Mulumba have always been somewhat conservational. In crop husbandry, local people have traditionally practiced what is known as slash and burn. The farmer usually clears a small piece of land, about one acre, and leaves the stumps of trees and the larger severed branches. This practice controls erosion since the top soil is not removed by running water. After the land is cleared, and some of the cuts have dried, farmers burn the field and plant at the first rain. Usually several crops are planted in the same field; it is common to see farmers planting manioc while they are harvesting peanuts or planting beans while weeding corn. This multiple cropping always keeps something growing in the soil to protect it against the sun and the rain. The last crop in the rotation is manioc, which can stay in the ground for up to two years. After the manioc is harvested, the field is left fallow for about ten years to regenerate the soil.

In animal husbandry, the methods are also mostly conservational. The diet of people is not oriented towards meat (the people prefer fish and vegetables), so usually there are very few animals per person (less than one goat or one chicken per person). Animals eat the by-products of food processed for human consumption. For example, goats, sheep, and chickens are fed the by-products of processed manioc and corn. They also eat tree leaves, green grass, and in the case of chickens, worms and small insects. Generally speaking, the animals do not constitute an ecological danger. Even when they eat tree leaves, they eat only leaves that they can reach; they usually stay close to the village and do not forage in the wild.

Villagers also exploit the local wild game sparingly, which was not abundant in 1960. Usually they set traps to capture one animal at a time. When hunting rodents during the two-month hunting season, they use the three or four hunting dogs available in the village. Villagers rarely used bush fire—generally hazardous to the ecological system—as a hunting device.

The exploitation of natural vegetation is also conservational. Wild fruits are gathered in season. Only the fruits are picked from the bush; the bush is left to grow. Young children who gather these fruits do not affect the grass cover at all. Similarly, the cutting of palm nuts and wine tapping do not affect the life of the trees. Many of the trees which are tapped for wine, however, do not bear palm fruits since the male flowers are cut young, eliminating cross pollination. Furthermore, much of the sap of the tree is taken to drink.

The tree itself, however, continues to live. Damage to palm trees is limited by the difficulty of acquiring the necessary climbing skills. In order to climb well, one must begin at an early age and learn to use a special climbing belt. Only a small percentage of people (three or four out of 100) masters the art of climbing a palm tree; thus it is difficult to challenge the environment through the aggressive harvesting of palm fruits.

The grass used for thatch is cut with a machete or pulled by hand; either technique leaves about five centimeters of grass on the ground. Although construction of houses requires many resources (sticks, thatch, and mud), houses last about ten years before they need to be replaced. The old branches removed from the razed homes are often used as firewood. Sometimes, though rarely, people cut fresh trees and leave them on the ground to dry for several weeks.

Traditional methods of exploiting water-based resources are also conservational, with a few exceptions. Fishing is done with catches (like lobster baskets) or with lines. Catches capture several fish or several kinds of fish at one time, but rarely more than four fish in one catch during a good season. Sometimes a poison called *mbuba* is used in non-running water. Once every three years the women use a system whereby they dam the river and dry the waterbed to expose the fish for catching. This process often takes an entire day, but the waterbed usually remains dry for only one or two hours since the dam is not very effective in holding back the water. Generally speaking, the traditional ways of exploiting this natural system do not constitute a serious threat to the environment.

## New Forms and the Rate of Utilization

The mission station seems to have had a directly negative impact on the local environment. First, the mission introduced a new form of land ownership (private property) and reduced the land available to the community by about one-third. This consequently reduced the length of time in which a field remained fallow and contributed to soil erosion. New techniques of land exploitation that cleared trees more effectively (removal of stumps and roots) led to a loss of about 50,000 trees. (The local trees take an average of thirty years to reach maturity.) Secondly, the construction of modern, Western buildings required 50,000 to 100,000 trees to bake 500,000 to 1,000,000 bricks. In addition, some of these new buildings were constructed with local materials such as thatch and trees. Thirdly, the presence of the station increased the consumption of home energy in the form of firewood: an expatriate population of about six families used almost 10,000 trees a year for fuel; about fifty families on the station needed about 20,000 trees a year; and Bakwa Mulumba villagers used more than 40,000 trees a year. Another 25,000 to 50,000 trees were needed to construct houses for the local population at the station. This housing also required 5,000 to 10,000 square meters of land; about another 500,000 square meters of land went into field use. The extra space needed for housing the station's local population possibly contributed to a further reduction of fallow time and an increase in soil loss and erosion. This tremendous and rapid increase in the consumption of ground cover exposed the soil to sun, wind, and rain—increasing its erosion and destroying its structure.

In addition to these direct impacts, the Kalonda Station may have had an indirect impact on the ecological system of the village of Bakwa Mulumba. Two aspects of the station are relevant here. First, the Western school espoused Western materialistic values, including the desire for Western material goods, but did not provide any skills for making the goods or the money needed to buy them. The traditional agricultural work became devalued; no agricultural skills were taught in the school that would help children to survive in their own culture. Without the means to earn a living, school-educated people—filled with Western consumer expectations—turned to diamond mining and trading in the hope of acquiring a lot of money quickly. Haphazard digging for diamonds dumped a lot of clay soil into the water, reducing the fish life. The school-oriented young people adopted a new kind of relation to their environment.

Secondly, evangelization may have affected the place that the environment enjoyed in the local culture. Several institutions linked to conservation of the environment and providing an opportunity for people to relate intimately to nature lost their prestige. Local religious beliefs encouraged people to plant trees and to conserve the natural environment. For example, people in Bakwa Mulumba have followed a religious tradition wherein they plant a small tree called *nkambua* to represent the spirit of the paternal grandmother. This tree is planted when a young man starts a household, when a married couple wants to have children, or when the family wants to give thanks to the ancestor's spirit. The ceremony itself includes an individual prayer, a petition to the spirit of the grandmother (*lusanzu*), and the killing of a chicken. Food is placed under the newly planted tree so that the ancestor will come to eat during the night. Usually the small tree is kept with some grass around it in an area of about ten square feet. The tree is of a hardy variety that almost always survives; it does not lose its leaves, and it has bark that resembles the cactus plant. This tree and the shrubs around it are easy to grow and provide a good protection for the soil.

*Mulemba* is another tree linked to a form of religious worship. In this case, it represents the spirit of ancestors who were political leaders. The peole of Bakwa Mulumba village believe that the qualities of political leadership and the responsibilities that come with such leadership are inherited. If, for some reason, one is not willing to recognize one's heritage, one may face the wrath of the ancestors. Thus, people who are related to the political leadership often have to plant the *mulemba* tree. The ceremony here includes a *lusanzu* and a talk with deceased ancestors. A goat is killed and some meat is placed under the tree as food for the ancestors. The tree used in this ritual looks like a rubber tree; it is always green, has deep roots, never fails to grow, gives much shade, and is easily incorporated into the local architecture.

*Mulemba* is also related to burial rites. For instance, when a man dies, especially one who is related to the political leadership, a *mulemba* tree is planted on his tomb in the yard of his home. Then a vine is tied to his finger and put around the *mulemba* tree. The tree and the vine grow together. Initially there were no ceremonies in the Bakwa Mulumba village, thus only a few *mulemba* trees stood. Palm trees also play a role in a burial ceremony. They are used to build the small shelter in which the body is laid out before the actual burial. These trees prevent erosion and have the many practical uses mentioned above.

Other rites involving trees are linked to birth rather than death. Four of them are especially notable. Traditionally, banana leaves are used to receive children when they are born. The banana tree also figures prominently in anoter rite called *tshibota tshia ku diyala*. When a child is born a banana tree is planted in the yard, and then for two years the child's stools are thrown around the bottom of the tree. Usually, the banana tree grows well because of the manure. If the family is large, a small garden of banana trees grows behind the house. The third rite involves *mwabi*, the tree of luck. This tree is planted in the court when a child is born in order to ward off jealous spirits who may try to kill the child. The fourth birth rite involving trees has to do with premature children. When a child is born prematurely, the parents plant a tree called *tshisanga-sanga* in addition to the customary banana tree. The *tshisanga-sanga* belongs to the same family as the *nsanga* tree, which is a symbol of strength and is associated with the place of origin of the Luba people — including Bakwa Mulumba. All these trees contribute to the environment and provide the people with a sense of strength. In addition, the banana trees are a valuable source of food.

Aside from specific rites, many beliefs in Bakwa Mulumba attribute spiritual healing power to the natural environment, as in the case of premature children. Sometimes spiritual and physical healing for adults is gained by staying close to nature. Some people build small houses in the bush when they are sick in order to regain their health. Others build small huts in the bush to stay for several weeks or months in order to accomplish a particular work, or just to have inner peace.

Trees and the natural environment occupy an important role in the life of the people. This holds for all major transitions: death, birth, passage to adulthood, illness, and recovery. Generally, in their culture, people identify with trees as major natural forces—referred to as *Kazadi Mutsi, diku dia mutshi*. Many aspects of life are related to the maintenance of trees around the house. Some Christian teachings or values, however, may have undermined the ecological aspects of the local society by undermining the traditional beliefs

In some instances, Christian teachings may have had a negative impact on the traditional religious practices mentioned above. Christianity teaches that God is in heaven and that no other intermediary between God and humans exists other than Jesus Christ. Local culture, on the other hand, believes that God is the oldest of the ancestors. Continuity, not rupture, exists between God and the living through the dead ancestors, who are perceived as intermediaries. The rites of *mulemba wa bukelenga*, as they relate to ancestors, contradict Christianity. When someone becomes a Christian, he or she is required to abandon all ancestor worship practices.

Also, Christianity traditionally recognizes the existence of Satan, God, Jesus as the Son of God, and the Holy Spirit; no room exists for spirits in nature. Christian teachers assert that beliefs about spirits in nature are superstitious.

Another instance of the negative impact of Christian teaching on local environment has to do with the Western notion of hygiene. Christian educators taught people that having too many trees around brought snakes and mosquitoes. People were instructed to live in a clean environment. Since snakes tend to be shy of people, the incidence of snakebite had, in fact, always been extremely low. Paradoxically, more mosquitoes could be found in modern homes than in the traditional ones since the smoke from fires in the latter repelled mosquitoes. Western medicine displaced the traditional medicine that linked humans to the spirits in the trees and plants. People began to trust more in the dispensaries and the hospitals than in the healing principles of their natural environment. As a result of the Christian education brought in by the church, people had fewer incentives to conserve trees and the rest of nature around them. Consequently, they may have caused the soil and land in general to deteriorate.

## Conclusion

Because of the tragic African food crisis and the prospect of future crises, traditional African land management techniques have come under criticism. Bush fire, overgrazing, and deforestation have become common words in the description of the local management traditions. At the same time, the work of church agencies has been perceived as good (and sometimes, almost holy). Many assume that churches—unlike large corporations that exploit huge quantities of natural resources (oil, minerals)—do not create environmental problems. It is assumed that church projects tend to be small and deal mostly with evangelization, education, and relief. Even though there are many cases in which these assumptions are correct, in some cases they are false. The case of Bakwa Mulumba village and the Kalonda mission station proves that a church project can have destructive effects on the environment, including the reduction of grass cover, the decline of trees, and the consequential deterioration of water quality. Such effects are likely to create profound changes in the life of the local community such as a reduction of agricultural activities, fishing, wine tapping, and animal raising. While both the church and local practices contributed to the degradation of the ground cover and the subsequent soil erosion, clearly the church station may have played a greater role in the above ecological problem than did traditional management practices. The assumption that local practices cause the environment to deteriorate does not seem to hold. On the contrary, it appears that most local practices helped to conserve the environment. Slash and burn techniques, used with a long fallow period and multiple cropping, kept the soil from being eroded and gave it the opportunity to regenerate. Methods of animal husbandry restricted animals to the village and fed them, in part, on the remains of human food. Hunting of wild game was limited; fishing techniques caught selected kinds of fish, except in the case of *kutuwa* or *mbuba* (which were rarely practiced).

In contrast, church projects seem to have had a negative impact on the local ecological situation. A large number of trees and grass were used in short periods of time without conservation measures. Through educational and evangelization programs, church projects undermined both the local economy and local religious beliefs. The former brought dependence on the international market, and the latter may have caused a loss of reverence for the natural environment.

The case of Bakwa Mulumba village does more than challenge the assumption that church projects do not have a negative impact on the environment; it also suggests that we should adopt policies and attitudes in planning that would enhance the relation of the church projects to their local environments. Four broad guidelines should be followed in order to promote a more ecologically responsible form of missionary work:

1) Make an environmental assessment of the projected church action.

2) Outline some remedial actions that can be taken in the case negative impacts occur; for each action include some details about long-term costs and benefits to the local community.

3) Determine what specific values and behaviors in the local community promote or hinder a better relation with the environment.

4) Design specific policies to encourage and promote the values mentioned above and finally to stimulate the people to protect their own life support system. This can be done with a sense of continuity and respect for the established wisdom of traditional ecological practices.

## Chapter 5

# Integrated Holistic Development and the World Mission of the Church

*by James W. Gustafson*

Traditionally speaking, the world mission of the church has been narrowly defined in terms of spiritual rather than social human needs. It has dealt with the salvation of the soul with only minimal concern for the salvation of the body. It has addressed physical, social, or economic needs by setting up separate organizations to deal with them. While the missions supposedly do the real missionary (spiritual) work, the relief and development organizations do the socio-economic (secular) work.

The church today manifests an increasing interest in socio-economic needs. Relief and development organizations are many and growing, raising the issue of the relationship of evangelism to socio-economic ministries in many churches. In spite of interest in the subject, however, little or no movement exists to do the world mission of the church in a holistic and integrated way. The world mission of the church is, biblically speaking, a mission to whole persons and to the whole creation, and the failure of the church to implement this insight reveals the gulf still existing between theology and practice.

Since 1977, we have been struggling with the implications of the holistic mission of the church in Udon, Thailand. We are doing what we call "integrated holistic development." It is *development* in that it seeks to transform people from what they are to what they are meant to be in Christ. It is *holistic* in that it deals with whole persons and all areas of their lives. It is *integrated* in that all aspects of the ministry are tied together and could not exist or function independently.

## An Overview

Our integrated holistic development ministry began (in 1977) with the establishment of the Center for Church Planting and Church Growth in northeast Thailand. Its original purpose was to plant "contextualized dynamic equivalent" churches in northeast Thailand, the poverty belt of that country. Since that time, the Center and its ministry have grown. It has given birth to over 100 churches and has started the Issan Development Foundation to deal with the socio-economic needs of the people of northeast Thailand. Today the Center and the Foundation are pioneering the contextualization of the gospel in theology, music, dance, and drama, and the contextualization of the church in faith, practice, and lifestyle. They are promoting the integration of social and spiritual ministry, including the development of local ecosystems or integrated farming systems. The basic goal of the Center and Foundation is to establish groups of people in the process of being transformed, churches that are integrated into society, culture, and Nature.

The Center and the Foundation are operated by the same staff. The Center focuses on church-related ministries, such as church planting, church enablement, music, song, and dance (See Appendix 1). The Foundation is concerned with the social and economic ministries to the church, such as pig banks, rice banks, eco-system co-ops, and community health and welfare (See Appendix 4). The foundation exists as an official organization recognized by the Thai government. It is capable of owning land and representing those persons who have legal problems. These two organizations have been set up out of legal necessity. Spiritual work cannot officially be mixed into the Foundation and still be accepted by the government. In fact, however, both the Center and the Foundation are integrated in the sense that the same goals, policies, and people govern both organizations. Functionally, they are two arms of the same body.

An important part of the Foundation is the Udon Patina farm, a thirty-acre, farming system that integrates rice mill, fish, pigs, ducks, chickens, trees, and vegetables (See Appendixes 3 and 4). The farm exists for a number of important reasons: 1) as the economic support base for all expenses of the Center and Foundation; 2) as the resource center for support, materials, and technology for all socio-economic development projects; 3) as the basic model for all ecosystem cooperative projects done at the village level; and 4) as an agricultural implementation center. Nothing is introduced at the village level before being tested at the farm first.

The Center and Foundation (including the farm) work together in an integrated way to establish new communities, help them grow in a new relationship to God, humanity, and nature, and to develop a dynamic new life-style in response to God's grace (See Appendix 1).

## Core Values

Robert H. Waterman Jr., the president if IBM, has written concerning the importance of beliefs or values in the success of any organization:

I firmly believe that any organization in order to survive and achieve success must have a sound set of beliefs on which it premises all its policies and actions. Next I believe that the most important single factor in corporate success is faithful adherence to those beliefs. And, finally, I believe if an organization is to meet the challenge of a changing world, it must be prepared to change everything about itself except those beliefs, as it moves through corporate life.[1]

What Waterman has said about values in the management of business organizations and values applies just as well to the Christian church. We have identified three basic values at the core of our whole ministry in northeast Thailand, values that must persevere through all our experiments: 1) the authority of the Word of God in Christ as the work of grace; 2) the integration of all aspects of life and work under God's grace; and 3) the flexibility to change any form of work or organization to communicate more clearly the grace of God.

A number of theological assumptions acts as a foundation to our concept of integrated holistic development. We believe that the whole of God's creation is under the curse of sin and is suffering as a result of this condition. Sin affects the whole of human life, causing us to labor to eat, to fight disease and decay constantly, and to live governed by a self-centeredness that prompts us to take advantage of the rest of creation for our own selfish motives. Even nature suffers from disease, decay, and destruction.

This state of affairs has resulted from and results in a severing of relationships—between God and God's creation, between human beings, and between humanity and the rest of creation. The universal need of all creation is thus to be put back into right relationship with God (the Creator), with humanity, and with nature. By God's grace in Jesus Christ, humanity is reconciled to God and creation, and at the deepest level our values and mind-sets are transformed. The church of Jesus Christ is an agent of this reconciliation, anticipated in its fulfillment at the second coming of Jesus Christ. In the meantime, it is the church's responsibility to work toward this reconciliation and transformation, here and now, by the power of God's grace.

Integrated holistic development is the system we have been devising in northeast Thailand for doing the gospel as an agent of reconciliation. This includes a variety of things: church planting; theological education; leadership training; biblical study; management training; agricultural research and training; preventative medicine; health and hygiene training; contextualized music; song and dance development; socio-economic programs; economic support base development; and more.

## The Process of Integrated Holistic Development

Integrated holistic development is a lifelong process and is progressive in nature. Its focus is the development of the total person. It emphasizes the functional relationship between the various aspects of true spiritual, physical, psychological, social, and economical development. It results in the development of the natural creation by people who have been and are being transformed by the renewal of their minds in Jesus Christ. Only such people can do comprehensive and consistent integrated holistic development. The best innovators are local people within a community who are being transformed as they experience integrated holistic development themselves.

The process of integrated holistic development takes place in seven basic steps. While there is a certain sequence necessary in the steps, each of them is in continual process. None of them is ever completed, but remains part of a vibrant and vital mix. These are practical rather than theoretical points, all of which are the essential ingredients of our organizational life-style in Udon.

## 1. Know the message of the gospel.

The first principle of integrated holistic development is that those practicing it must understand and accept the essence of the gospel (God's grace in Jesus Christ) and experience the transforming power of God in their lives (a transformation of value systems).

The gospel is God's power to salvation (Rom 1:10 and 17). Put another way, the gospel is God's power to transform people at the value and belief system level. We believe in the renewal of the world by God in Jesus Christ. The work of integrated holistic development is God's work from start to finish. We have no confidence in progress through human achievement or in the underlying idea that human beings are basically good. Rather, our concept of human being is that we are basically weak and incapable of working for the good of others or the creation. Humans are fundamentally self-centered and, thus, deny the greatness of God and the importance of others and the creation.

The act of God in Jesus Christ can change persons and provide the power for new life—power for a basic value system change (Rom 12:2). Integrated holistic development is concerned with the confrontation of human value systems with the new value system of God. It is concerned with the new life-style that results from a transformation of the human mind-set and with the results of this process of transformation for the larger community of humankind and creation.

The gospel message is that there is no one good but God (Luke 18:19). This goodness (righteousness) of God is free as a gift to all who believe and accept it (Eph 2:8–9). It is the power of God (Rom 1:16–17) that will utterly transform humanity and enable it to become what God originally planned it to be.

## 2. Know the local people and the local culture.

The second basic principle is that integrated holistic development requires a deep understanding of the people and local culture being addressed.

On a secular level, I have seen development schemes by well-meaning organizations fail because they do not understand the northeast Thai villagers and their culture. Westerners, especially, like to believe that all people think as they do. Nothing could be further from the truth.

Knowing a language is not enough; knowing what persons mean by what they say is even more crucial. One may understand the Thai language and yet not understand the mind-set or the values of a Thai. Knowing the mind-set and values of people is essential for beginning where they are.

For example, some well-meaning Christians have tried to persuade certain Thai to admit that they are sinners. Because the Thai culture gives great weight to shame, this effort is usually repudiated. On the one hand, the Thai are locked into a legalistic religious system of gaining merit by not sinning, and on the other hand, they know that any admittance of sin would bring the loss of face in the eyes of society. The question is how to get the Thai to sense their need of the help that only God can give. Our answer—after much study both of the Bible and of the Thai value system—is to redefine sin. Instead of accepting that sin is doing bad things (as many traditional Christians believe), we have defined sin as "egocentrism" and the "selfish nature of humans." A basic value of Thai culture is "I am the source of dependence for myself." Two corollaries are "to each his own" and "I can't see anyone but myself as good." Most Thai will subscribe to the axiom *"hen kae tua"* ("look out only for self"). Thus, the definition of sin as egocentrism hits home and also encounters a positive response. When they have been helped to think through the implications of their current value system, their question is generally "What can I do?" The answer is the gospel message that only God can do anything to help you and that God has helped in Jesus Christ. Then they can be confronted with the value system of the gospel: "Love your neighbor as you love yourself!" One must know the local culture and mind-sets of the people in order to evaluate the progress of transformation in their minds and attitudes. We may readily think that everything is going well because people are doing things according to a project or program we have laid out. But we should consider whether they have actually begun to be transformed in the area of mind-sets and values or are merely parroting the Christian system for personal gain? (See Appendix 2 for other comparisons of Thai and biblical values.)

Successful transformation takes time, effort, and the capacity to pull oneself out of one's own cultural grid and immerse oneself in another cultural situation. Generally, we have failed to do this and have, instead, developed a Christianity around the world that is basically Western in focus. We do not really speak to the people and the local culture. We develop local followers who are removed from the local culture and who have become like us—which we interpret as Christian, rather than Thai or some other non-Christian culture. As the head of the Thai immigration department in Bangkok once told me: "Missionaries never listen and never try to learn who we are and what we are. They are always trying to tell us something. I feel that missionaries are the most selfish people I know!"

## 3. Contextualize the message of the gospel.

To be understood clearly, the gospel message must be phrased in the local forms, expressions, and idioms of the receptor culture. In this way, the message of the gospel can be contextualized (incarnated) into that local setting.

People can communicate clearly only to the extent that they share a common culture. As a result, communication takes place best when two participants (the source and the receptor) and the message (the gospel) are part of the same culture. Communication is what is heard, however, not what is said. Communication, itself, cannot transfer meaning, only information. Meaning takes place in the mind of the receptor and conforms to his or her cultural grid. Effective communication must, therefore, be receptor-oriented so that the receptors receive the message and experience its relationship to life as they live and understand it.

A false fear abounds that expressing the gospel in the forms of a local culture will create a syncretistic and, therefore, non-Christian movement. In fact, Christianity around the world is largely Western in forms and expressions but houses the value system of the local culture in those forms and expressions. What we currently have is a Christianity that is highly syncretistic and non-Christian in its values and belief system.

In contrast, integrated holistic development emphasizes what we have called dynamic equivalence versus the formal correspondence espoused by much of the church today. Formal correspondence places emphasis on the formal aspects of Western Christianity. In the transmission of Christianity to other countries, the form and expressions stay the same. There is correspondence of form between both the sender and the receptor cultures. The problem is that in countries such as Thailand, Thai Christianity parrots the forms of Western Christianity and retains the values and beliefs of the local culture.

Dynamic equivalence places emphasis on the context or message to be communicated and seeks to use local forms and expressions that are capable of communicating this message. The goal is to do whatever is necessary to make sure the original message is faithfully rephrased in functionally equivalent words, idioms, and forms of the receptor culture. In dynamic equivalence the form changes, but the message stays the same.

We have attempted to develop a northeast Thai Christian community (church) that, in its forms and expressions, is completely identified with its context. Our language is *Lao* (heart language of the northeast); our hymns are northeast Thai tunes with scripture; our ceremonies are northeast Thai ceremonies impregnated with the gospel; our liturgy is drawn from the northeast Thai social context and used to express glory to God. Our people dance in worship services to express glory to God. There is no preaching, but rather a discussion centered on the Bible and led by elders asking questions about a passage. There are no church buildings; we meet in houses. We have adopted many of the northeast traditions into the life-style of the church, such as tying strings in love and blessing.

The response on the part of the traditional Thai church has been everything from disbelief to dismay. We have been accused of being demonic by some fellow Christians, and our salvation has been questioned by others. We are rocking the cultural boat of traditional Christianity in Thailand. Those who listen long enough to understand that what we are doing is contextualization voice support. When questioned about why they are not doing similar things, however, they shake their heads and say that, although their organizations give lip service to contextualization, they would never dare actually do it.

## 4. Confront the value system of the local culture with that of the gospel.

Every effort must be made to contrast the value system of the local culture with that of the gospel.

The true value system of the gospel is constantly at loggerheads with the value system of all societies. The first step, therefore, in confronting the value system of a local culture with the value system of the gospel is to study the value system of the gospel. The uniqueness of the value system of the gospel is immediately apparent. The gospel says: if you want to be great, then serve; if you want to be first, be last; if you want to live, die; if you want to be strong, be weak; if you want to be good, admit you're bad; do not curse, but bless; do not take, but give; do not love yourself only, but love your neighbor as you love yourself.

The second step in confronting the value system of a local culture with the value system of the gospel is to study the value system of the local culture. The easiest way—and perhaps the least helpful—is to study books written by foreign researchers (anthropologists and sociologists) on the value system of local cultures. This is good background material and serves to acquaint one with the mind-set of the local culture. The weakness of studies done by Western social scientists, however, is their seeming inability to grapple honestly with the truth of the value systems of local cultures. Western social scientists are most often trying to prove or disprove certain theoretical assumptions of their own; this keeps them from seeing things that do not fit into their theoretical grid. Combined with this is the natural reticence of most Western social scientists to say anything negative about a given culture for fear of seeming to lose their objectivity. This reluctance often leads to the neglect of important aspects of the value system of a given culture.

A second approach to understanding the local cultural value system is to read studies done by nationals and written in the language of the local culture. They tend to be more open and honest, providing valuable insights.

A third way to gain insight into the value systems of the local culture is through personal observation and discussion with local people. I have found this to be the most productive. Before this can be done, however, the trust of the local people must be won so that they will ever open up and describe the local context honestly.

## 5. Establish dynamic equivalent churches in the local culture.

Churches that live out the new value system of the gospel in their own local communities while retaining the local cultural forms and expressions (dynamic equivalence churches) must be established.

These churches are the new community of the gospel. They maintain their relationship to the old community and so become innovators from within. They are doing the gospel of grace in Jesus Christ in their own local cultural setting. They are expressing and living the gospel in a way that would appear foreign to outsiders, but is clear to insiders. They are enabling the gospel to impregnate their culture and confront values and mind-sets so that their people and culture may be transformed by its power. They are dynamically equivalent in belief and practice to all churches that are firmly based on the gospel, yet they are formally different from all churches in other cultures.

## 6. Establish socio-economic projects in dynamic equivalent churches.

Socio-economic projects must be set up that provide the church with an economic support base, a lab for spiritual development, a resource center for doing integrated holistic development in the community, and a tangible means of expressing the grace of God in Jesus Christ to their community.

Once groups of people who are being transformed by the grace of God are united as a dynamic equivalence church, the socio-economic aspect of the work is begun. A number of basic principles are central to the socio-economic development aspect of integrated holistic development.

The church alone is the focal point of all our socio-economic development work—for several reasons. Successful work is ultimately impossible within a non-Christian value system. The church is the ideal agent of integrated holistic development (including socio-economic development) because no agency is better suited for doing this work in any culture (especially not Western relief and development organizations). As a resource center for integrated holistic development in the local community, the local church can facilitate development faster and more comprehensively than socio-economic development projects done by Western organizations. The latter's efforts with non-Christians in the local culture are not only nonproductive but destructive to the church of Jesus Christ in those areas. Finally, we do not have the materials, facilities, or management capability to work with anyone else but the church. Our churches are growing so rapidly that we cannot even keep up with the socio-economic development needs of our own groups. Today we have projects in only twenty-five out of a total of 136 churches. Rather than include the non-Christian element of the community as well, it is more efficient to equip the local church to do the work.

The socio-economic aspect of our ministry is not a separate operation from the rest of the work (with an evangelist or two thrown in to make it appear to be Christian), but rather is integrated totally with the other aspects of our work.

The socio-economic development projects enable the local church members to raise their standard of living—not an end in itself, but rather a means to the end of good stewardship. Because the local church members have experienced God's grace in the development project and are economically better off, they now have the means to tithe and give to God part of what they have been given. These offerings go directly to the local church, and the church body is able to use these funds for the partial support of the church. Traditionally, one of the most difficult things for the Christian church to do in northeast Thailand has been to get church members to tithe. In integrated holistic development, however, a person receives (by God's grace) and then is encouraged to give in a response of gratitude to God.

In all the socio-economic projects, the church has one share of all profits (equal to one family). The tithe and gifts of the members are over and above this share. For example, in the pig bank project, each member has two pigs. The church also has two pigs. If anyone quits the project before its completion, his or her share (both profits and capital funds) goes to the church. These funds are used by the member to support the expenses of the local church (helping the sick and poor, travel to meetings and seminars, or supporting elders and pastors in the future if they so choose).

The socio-economic development projects are also labs for spiritual development. They provide the context in which the members of the local church can grow spiritually. All of the development projects are communally-oriented cooperatives. They each require people to work together, sharing the work and the profits. For northeast Thai, who rarely cooperate, this is a difficult system. The normal reaction of groups after a month of working on the project is that "we can't do this at all." Our response is to say that they are absolutely right and that the only one who can do it is God. This again encourages the group to return to the spiritual foundation of God's grace and the enabling power that comes from it. The development projects are problem starters, but these very problems are the actual points of spiritual growth, if dealt with in a way consistent with the grace of God in Jesus Christ.

The socio-economic projects become resource centers for the spontaneous expansion of the church into society. The church itself can reach out and touch its community only if it has the resources to do so. Churches that are part of the integrated holistic development process have the needed resources (a transformed value system; an ability to study, understand, and apply the gospel; ducks; fish; pigs; trees; funds; and more). They also have the desire to reach out to minister to their own communities in a holistic way. Most importantly, their communities will respond positively to such a holistic movement from within the community when they would, no doubt, have rejected a spiritually-oriented evangelistic effort from without.

The development projects provide the local church with a tangible way to show the *agape* love of Jesus Christ, which is the life-style of the being-transformed-church (based on the new value system of the gospel). To tell people that God loves them and to be unable to meet their felt needs appear ridiculous in the eyes of those who are scraping the bottom and have nothing.

The socio-economic development projects strive to help the members understand the natural creation (which they have abused all of their lives) and their relationship and responsibility to it.

We use an ecosystem approach to doing integrated farming. We are trying to bring together into one ecosystem model as many aspects of agriculture in northeast Thailand as possible. This approach does a number of things. It provides an efficient and productive integrated farming system, which is more likely to provide a good support base than a one-type-only farming set up such as rice (See Appendix 3). The ecosystem model shows relationships within creation. As the members learn this, they begin to understand the relatedness of all of God's creation, including themselves. It shows that we can manage and improve nature through good management and a sound understanding of how it works. This model provides the knowledge and motivation for helping the members reverse their old value system and reach out to restore the land of the northeast (robbed for countless years by human exploitation and manipulation) to what it should be in God's plan.

## 7. Enable the church to do integrated holistic development in its own community.

The end result of integrated holistic development is the spontaneous movement of the church out into its community.

The church, itself, has become what we call a resource center for integrated holistic development. It has received input from all areas of our holistic ministry and has resource people being trained in all of these areas. The church is equipped to reach out into its local culture and allow the grace of God to begin to do the work of transforming people, society, and nature into what they are each meant to be in Jesus Christ.

## Conclusion

Our conviction, based on experience, is that if the church of Jesus Christ can understand the gospel, understand the local people and the culture it addresses, contextualize the gospel message into the forms and expressions of the local culture, confront the local value system with the value system of the gospel, establish dynamic equivalence churches, establish socio-economic development projects in the local churches, and enable the local church to do integrated holistic development in its own community, then the world mission of the church will begin to turn people, culture, and the creation rightside up (as they are meant to be) by the grace of God in Jesus Christ.

## Notes

[1]Thomas J. Peters and Robert H. Waterman, Jr., eds., *In Search of Excellence* (New York: Warner Books, 1983) 280.

# Appendix 1

*Diagram*

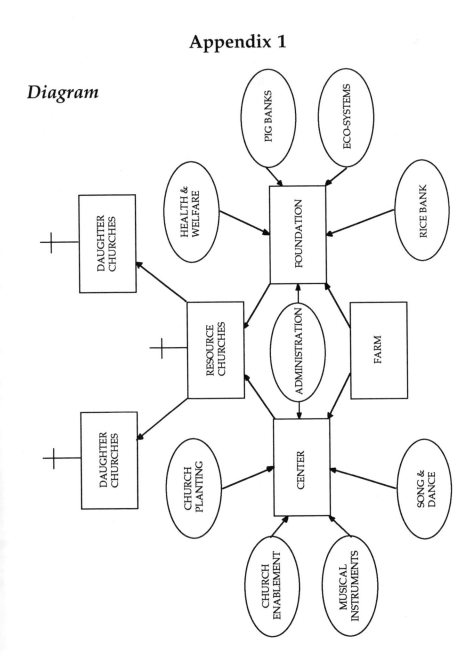

## Notes

The following is a summary of the individual components of the diagram on the preceding page. All aspects or parts of the above integrated system work together to do the task of integrated holistic development. No aspect of the above integrated system could be deleted without severely limiting the total ministry.

**1. FARM**     (Exists to provide financial support for the Center and Foundation)

- Provides financial support for all Center and Foundation overhead costs.

- Provides materials (pigs, fish, ducks, and trees) for all Development projects.

- Agricultural experimentation center (adapting agricultural technology to the northeast).

- Model for all development projects: how to do it at the village level.

**2. CENTER**   (Exists to plan and enable churches to be strong in northeast Thailand)

- Church Planting: plants churches, stabilizes them and teaches church planting elders to do the same with daughter churches.

- Church Enablement: Trains elders both to lead in their own church (pastor) and to train elders in daughter churches to do the same.

- Musical Instruments: Trains instrumentalists both to lead in their own churches (instruments) and to train instrumentalists in daughter churches to do the same.

- Song and Dance: Trains song leaders to lead in their own church (songs) and to train song leaders in daughter churches to do the same.

- Administration: Trains deacons to handle finances and money of their own church and to train deacons in daughter churches to do the same.

Note: Multiple leaders provide a team approach to management.

3. FOUNDATION   (Socio-Economic Development: exists to provide the church with firm economic support base)

- Pig Bank (market pigs): the first stage of establishing an economic support base for the church.

- Pig Bank (sows): the second stage of establishing an economic support base for the church.

- Ecosystem co-ops: the third stage of establishing an economic support base for the church.

- Rice Bank: aims at relieving the debts incurred by church people over the years.

- Community Health: a preventative program that deals with health at the level of theology, culture, and health technology.

Note: These Development projects are not separate (independent) projects, but are integrally integrated with our whole ministry to the church. These projects

1) Provide better standard of living for individuals in the church.

2) Provide economic support base for the church.

3) Provide "lab" for spiritual development of the church.

4) Provide materials and funds for church movement into society.

5) Provide leadership support funds.

6) Provide funds for establishing and enabling "daughter" churches.

**4. RESOURCE CHURCHES**   (The result of church planting efforts from the Center.)

• The focus of all Center efforts at enabling and equipping the church.

• The focus of all Foundation efforts at providing a firm economic support base for the church.

• The resource center for extending Center and Foundation enabling and equipping to all "daughter" churches (diffusion).

**5. "DAUGHTER" CHURCHES** (The result of church planting efforts on the part of the "resource" church.)

• Receives all enablement from "resource" church (not Center or Foundation).

• In its turn it too becomes a "resource" church and plants "daughter" churches.

• Its "ministries" then become enabler and equippers for the new daughter churches (equipping "ministers" in the new daughter churches).

# Appendix 2

## Northeast Thai Values versus Biblical Values

| Northeast Thai Values | Biblical Values |
|---|---|
| 1. Basic focus is self. (*Hen kae tua yak pen yai.*) Concern is to help self alone. Looking out for one's own good is supported by society and religion. | 1. Basic focus is God and others. Concern is to help others. |
| 2. Personal ease and convenience. (*Kwam saduak suan tua.*) If not easy or convenient will not do it. | 2. Service oriented. Concern is how can I help others? |
| 3. To each his own. (*Tua krai tua man.*) I do my thing and you do yours. | 3. Community oriented. Cooperation within the group is a key value. |
| 4. Do not like to see others as good. (*Kee echa—hen kon eun dee mai dai.*) Jealousy predominates. | 4. Love others as love self. |

5. Dishonesty in relations.
(*Nah wai lung lok; Nam koon wai nai/ Nam sai wai nok.*)
Poor communication (do not   say what they think.)

5. Honesty in all relationships.
Let yes be yes and no be no.

6. Power for self is ultimate goal.
(*Kaw hai pen chaow pen nai.*)
Status and position: others serve you.

6.Weakness for self is goal of Christian; creates dependence on God.
In our weakness is God's strength.

7. Self is source of dependence.
(*Tua eng pen tee peung kong tua eng.*)

7. God is only true source of dependence.
Humans are weak and cannot be  depended upon.

8. Do not take responsibility easily.
(*Mai aow ching aow chung.*)
Like fun, not work.

8. Faithful in responsibility.
Goal is faithfulness, not personal ease.

9. Do good, get good;
do bad, get bad.

9. No one can do good enough to get good. All persons are weak sinners.

10. Love face and name in society.

10. Give God glory in society.

11. To each according to merit.
(works oriented)

11. To each according to need
(grace oriented)

# Appendix 3

## The Integrated Ecosystem Farm Model

A. The system integrates a number of different natural elements to form a functioning whole in nature.

B. Our elements are: rice, pigs, ducks, fish, chickens, vegetables, and trees.

C. These natural elements are integrated as follows:

1. The rice mill provides cracked rice and both soft and hard bran that are the basic ingredients of our pig feed. The rice mill also provides total resources for the ricebank project.

2. The pigs eat feed we prepare using rice and bran from the rice mill. The pigs in turn provide manure for the development of the rest of the ecosystem. The pigs also provide total resources for the pig bank co-op program as well as provide funds for the larger part of Center support.

3. The ducks are fed pig waste products (both manure and spilled feed) only. The ducks process the twenty percent or more of unprocessed nutrients in the pig manure. They in turn provide manure resources (five kilos of droppings a month per duck) which go straight into the fish ponds. They also provide total resources for the use of ducks in the co-op program.

4. The fish (ten different varieties) process both the pig and duck manure in different ways. Some varieties of fish eat the manure directly (common carp, walking catfish, channel catfish, tilapia). Other varieties eat the phytoplankton that feed on the fertilizer in the manure (silver carp, tawes). Still other varieties feed off of the zootoplankton which feeds on the phytoplankton (bighead carp). Other varieties feed on the aerobic and anaerobic bacteria produced in compost piles (Indian carp and common carp). One variety eats just vegetation (grass carp). One last variety kept for thinning out over-populated tilapia ponds eats mainly other fish (serpent head). The fish in turn provide water resources as well as fertilizer (dead fish) for the vegetable and tree project. The fish also provide total resources for the fish bank and co-op program as well as providing funds for a smaller part of Center support.

5. The vegetables and trees are watered with water from the fish ponds. All dead or waste fish are buried for fertilizer around the larger fruit trees. The fruit trees (bananas, katin, mangoes, coconuts, custart apple, papaya, and others) and the vegetables (kale, broccoli, Chinese cabbage, a variety of morning glory, etc.) are all planted on dikes. The vegetables and grass as well as the leaves of the katin tree provide natural feed for the fish (chopped up and thrown in the ponds green or mixed as compost). The vegetables and trees also provide total resources for the use of vegetables and trees in the co-op program.

6. The chickens process left over pig fed and pig manure. We are raising local breeds and experimenting with developing the best producing and most hardy breed. After we have determined the best breed, we will reintroduce that breed to our ecosystem coops. Chicken

droppings go into the ponds to fertilize the phyto-plankton there.

D. The elements form a functioning whole as depicted in the diagram below.

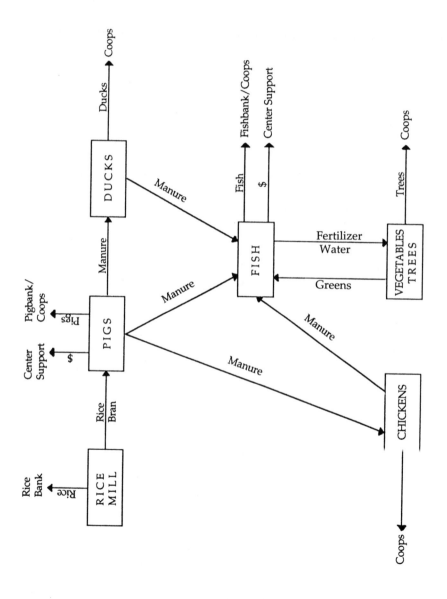

# Appendix 4

## Summary of Development Programs

### 1. THE RICE BANK PROJECT.

    a.  Basic resource: the rice mill.

        1)  The rice mill operates as a business. We buy in paddy and mill it for a profit.

        2)  The profits from the rice mill fund the rice bank program.

    b.  The rice bank program.

        1)  Provides milled rice for loan to needy farmers.

        2)  Loans (of rice) are given out to those meeting program conditions over a period from around May to December each year—a crucial period for farmers who have paid back exorbitant loans (400-500% interest) to local loan sharks in January (following harvest) and run out of rice to eat around May each year.

        3)  The rice bank supplies the farmers' basic rice needs over total period of need: rice mill "loans" the farmers milled rice at the rate of fifteen kilos an adult and ten kilos a child per month.

4) The farmers are required to pay back these loans in "paddy" in January (during harvest).

    a) There is no interest charged on the loan.

    b) 150 kilos paddy per 100 kilos of milled borrowed. (Paddy mills out to about sixty-five percent milled rice.)

5) A second function of the rice bank is to sell milled rice to needy farmers at wholesale prices (usually thirty percent or more below market prices) on a one month credit basis. This aspect of the rice bank program caters to the hired labor villager who has no land.

## 2. THE PIG BANK PROJECT

a. Basic resource: the pig farm

1) The pig farm operates as a business.

    a) We have 180 sows (fifteen boars) which are bred at the rate of thirty sows a month.

    b) 240 baby pigs are farrowed a month (eight per sow).

    c) The baby pigs are grown to a finished weight of 100 kilos and sold (240 per month) on the market.

2) The profits from the pig farm funds both the other Center and Foundation programs and the pig bank and coop project.

b. Pig bank program #1 ("Grower-finisher" program).

1) In the grower-finisher pig bank program the farmers are introduced to pig farming. They learn how to raise pigs for market over a two year period of time (five cycles of four to five months each).

2) Each family in the program is given two pigs (twelve to fifteen kilo weight each pig: These pigs are raised cooperatively with other members of the program in the same village. (In four to five months pigs are ready for market.)

3) The Foundation covers all the overhead costs of the program at first.

   a) Initial cost of the baby pigs.

   b) Cost of all feed stuff. (All feed is prepared at the farm and sent out to the farmers.)

   c) At sale (end of four to five months) the overhead costs are returned to the Foundation and the farmer gets profits.

4) The program slowly weans the farmer over the two year period.

   a) After the second five month cycle of raising pigs, twenty-five percent of overhead necessary for raising next cycle of pigs is deducted from the farmer's profit and invested for him by the Foundation.

b) After each subsequent cycle is finished twenty-five percent more is deducted until the farmer has built up 100 percent of a capital fund enabling him to raise the next cycle of pigs.

c) During the two year period the Foundation increasingly turns over the responsibility for managing the pigs to the farmer. (By the end of the two years the farmer is doing everything and the Foundation basically giving advice.)

5) After two years in the program the farmer has a capital fund and enough technical knowledge and experience to raise pigs on his own.

6) Each member gives ten percent of his total profits to the church.

a) These funds are re-invested in the pig bank (as above) with the profits going to the church.

b) Part of these profits will provide funding for the church's community development program in the future.

Note: In the five churches where this program was originally launched, each member raised four pigs and gave one to the church. In these villages the church now actually owns one pig for each original member. The Foundation was unable to continue the "four pig" program, however, due to the increasing number of members in the program and so now runs a "two pig" program.

c.  Pig bank program #2 (Sow program).

1) The "sow" program takes over after completion of the grower-finisher program, taking two years (four cycles of six months each) to complete.

2) This program has several objectives:

a)  To take the burden of providing baby pigs to farmers off the Foundation.

b)  To provide the farmers with a resource that would enable them to expand their grower-finisher programs as they are able. They can move from raising two pigs to market to three to four or more as they have baby pigs and funds available.

c)  To provide a resource base that will enable the church to reach out and start pig banks in the community they are in.

3) Each church group which has completed a "grower- finisher" program is loaned breed sows according to the number of grower-finishers needed. (One sow provides approximately eight babies or grower-finishers.)

4) The Foundation provides feed and medicine for the sow and babies up through weaning. It also provides breeding for the sow for the next cycle. At weaning the farmer returns enough baby pigs to the Foundation (value figured at market price) to cover the cost of feed and medicine for the cycle, one-fourth of the original cost of the sow, the cost of breeding the sow and twenty-five percent

of the overhead costs of the next cycle.

5) After two years the farmers have been weaned from the sow program.

a) They own the sows and have a capital fund for breeding the sows and raising the baby pigs to weaning. (The grower-finisher program takes over at this point.)

b) They have enough technical knowledge and experience to run a pig breeding program.

## 3. THE FISH BANK PROJECT

a. Basic resource: the fish ponds at the Farm.

1) The fish ponds operate as a business.

a) We are raising ten different kings of fish in various polycultures in thirty different ponds at the farm.

b) We spawn four of the breeds ourselves (tawes, common carp, walking catfish, tilapia) and sell the fingerlings as well as using them to stock our own ponds and the eco-system co-op ponds.

c) We seine the ponds, sell the fish and then restock the ponds on two different cycles:

(1) Chinese carp polyculture ponds: every six

months.

   (2) Tilapia polyculture ponds: every four
   months.

2) Both ducks and chickens are raised on some of the
   fish ponds adding enrichment to the ponds in the
   form of their droppings. The proceeds from the
   sale of ducks and chickens is considered part of the
   fish pond project.

3) The profits from the fish ponds fund both the other
   Center and Foundation programs in part and the
   fish bank and co-op project.

b. The fish bank program.

   1) The Foundation provides funding for digging fish
      ponds at the village level. The site must have been
      turned over to the local church and become com-
      munal property belonging to the whole group of
      Christians.

   2) The Foundation provides fish (tilapia: mono-
      culture) for stocking the ponds initially and train-
      ing in raising and harvesting the fish as well as
      chickens and ducks for pond enrichment.

   3) The farmers provide labor for finishing off the
      ponds and maintaining them after stocking.

   4) All profits from the ponds (fish or money) are
      divided equally by all members of the program.

      a) After the first three months the members take

daily catches from the ponds.

   b) Every four months the Foundation helps the farmers seine out the majority of the fish and restock.

5) After the first year of operation the farmers are required to give the original number of chickens, ducks, and fingerlings stocked in their pond to the local village community. The tilapia breeds naturally every three months. As a result, the farmers have an abundance of fingerlings at all times.

6) A new aspect of the fish bank project is the introduction of fruit trees (grown at the Foundation Farm) and vegetables to the dikes of the fish bank ponds. Compost from the pig manure and pond water provide the essential ingredients for growth.

## 4.  ECOSYSTEM COOPERATIVES

  a. The ecosystem cooperatives combine the pig bank and fish bank projects with a small rice mill (in trial stage now) into one integrated cooperative program.

   1) This "mini farm" is set up at the village level and is run by members of the local church community.

   2) It operates according to the rule of the individual projects as outlined above only combined into an ecosystem (as at the Farm).

   3) Co-op members share in the work and in the profits of the cooperative equally.

b. Importance of the ecosystem cooperative method.

1) The ecosystem cooperative provides a resource base for the church to improve its own standard of living and then reach out into its own community in holistic development. Gives the church the resources it needs to do the gospel.

2) The cooperative also provides an excellent "lab" in which the church can apply the truths of the value system of the gospel to their life-style.

   a) The old northeast Thai value system comes into vivid confrontation with the value system of God's Word in this program.

   b) Spiritual growth takes place as members work through the agony of cooperating, sharing, and coordinating themselves with others.

3) It also provides a model for the rest of the community at several levels.

   a) Life-style of those who are being "made new" and are rebuilding their lives on a new value system by the power of God.

   b) An example of how people with changed mind-sets (value systems) can develop in the socio-economic dimension. (socio-economic progress)

   c) A model of cooperation and other-centered concern possible in Christ that can change society radically.

# UDORN PATINA FARM

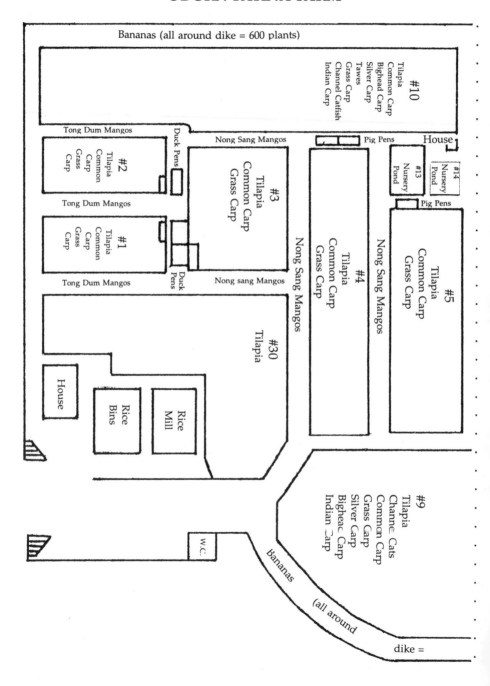

# Center for Church Planting and Church Growth in Northeast Thailand

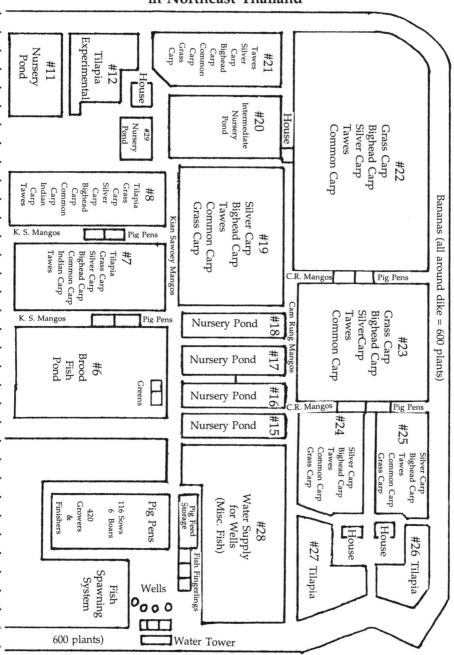

This is a publication of Au Sable Institute of Environmental Studies, an institution of higher education that provides courses and programs in Christian environmental stewardship and field ecology for college and university students worldwide, conducts an annual Au Sable Forum on Christianity and environment, provides environmental education for school children in the Institute's region, and helps individuals, churches, and denominations enhance Christian environmental stewardship in their lives and programs. Other publications originating from Au Sable Fora include *Tending the Garden: Essays on the Gospel and the Earth* (Wesley Granberg-Michaelson, ed.) and *The Environment and the Christian: What Can We Learn from the New Testament?* (Calvin B. DeWitt, ed.). Au Sable Institute is located in the northwoods country of Michigan's Lower Peninsula, about eighty miles southwest of the Straits of Mackinac and forty miles east of Traverse City, Michigan. It is licensed by the Department of Education of the State of Michigan and is a 501(c)3 not-for-profit corporation under the United States Internal Revenue Service Code. Inquiries on college courses, Au Sable Forum, programs, and service should be directed to 7526 Sunset Trail NE, Mancelona, Michigan 49659 or by phone to (616) 587-8686 or FAX to (608) 255-0950.